ALEXANDER POPE P

Alexander Pope (1688–
and translator. He publ
republished version of
Works were published
the *Odyssey* into Englis
famous works, was a vicious satire on Dullness featuring many
of his contemporaries.

John Fuller was educated at New College, Oxford, and was
formerly a Fellow and Tutor in English at Magdalen College. An
award-winning novelist, he has also published sixteen poetry
collections, the most recent of which is *The Space of Joy* (2006).
His *Collected Poems* appeared in 1996. John Fuller lives in
Oxford and is a Fellow of the Royal Society of Literature.

IN THE POET-TO-POET SERIES

W. H. AUDEN – Poems selected by John Fuller
WILLIAM BARNES – Poems selected by Andrew Motion
JOHN BERRYMAN – Poems selected by Michael Hofmann
JOHN BETJEMAN – Poems selected by Hugo Williams
WILLIAM BLAKE – Poems selected by James Fenton
ROBERT BROWNING – Poems selected by Douglas Dunn
ROBERT BURNS – Poems selected by Don Paterson
LORD BYRON – Poems selected by Paul Muldoon
THOMAS CAMPION – Poems selected by Charles Simic
GEOFFREY CHAUCER – Poems selected by Bernard O'Donoghue
JOHN CLARE – Poems selected by Paul Farley
SAMUEL TAYLOR COLERIDGE – Poems selected by James Fenton
HART CRANE – Poems selected by Maurice Riordan
EMILY DICKINSON – Poems selected by Ted Hughes
JOHN DONNE – Poems selected by Paul Muldoon
KEITH DOUGLAS – Poems selected by Ted Hughes
JOHN DRYDEN – Poems selected by Charles Tomlinson
ALLEN GINSBERG – Poems selected by Mark Ford
THOM GUNN – Poems selected by August Kleinzahler
THOMAS HARDY – Poems selected by Tom Paulin
GEORGE HERBERT – Poems selected by Jo Shapcott
ROBERT HERRICK – Poems selected by Stephen Romer
GERARD MANLEY HOPKINS – Poems selected by John Stammers
A. E. HOUSMAN – Poems selected by Alan Hollinghurst
TED HUGHES – Poems selected by Simon Armitage
JOHN KEATS – Poems selected by Andrew Motion
D. H. LAWRENCE – Poems selected by Tom Paulin
ROBERT LOWELL – Poems selected by Michael Hofmann
LOUIS MACNEICE – Poems selected by Michael Longley
ANDREW MARVELL – Poems selected by Sean O'Brien
WILFRED OWEN – Poems selected by Jon Stallworthy
SYLVIA PLATH – Poems selected by Ted Hughes
ALEXANDER POPE – Poems selected by John Fuller
EZRA POUND – Poems selected by Thom Gunn
WILLIAM SHAKESPEARE – Poems selected by Ted Hughes
JOHN SKELTON – Poems selected by Anthony Thwaite
WALLACE STEVENS – Poems selected by John Burnside
JONATHAN SWIFT – Poems selected by Derek Mahon
ALFRED, LORD TENNYSON – Poems selected by Mick Imlah
DYLAN THOMAS – Poems selected by Derek Mahon
WILLIAM WORDSWORTH – Poems selected by Seamus Heaney
THOMAS WYATT – Poems selected by Alice Oswald
W. B. YEATS – Poems selected by Seamus Heaney

ALEXANDER POPE

Poems selected by JOHN FULLER

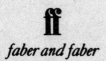

faber and faber

First published in 2008
by Faber and Faber Limited
3 Queen Square London WC1N 3AU

Photoset by RefineCatch Ltd, Bungay, Suffolk
Printed in England by CPI Bookmarque, Croydon

All rights reserved
Introduction and Selection © John Fuller, 2008

The right of John Fuller to be identified as editor
of this work has been asserted in accordance with Section 77
of the Copyright, Designs and Patents Act, 1988

*This book is sold subject to the condition that it shall not,
by way of trade or otherwise, be lent, resold, hired out or
otherwise circulated without the publisher's prior consent
in any form of binding or cover other than that in which
it is published and without a similar condition including this
condition being imposed on the subsequent purchaser*

A CIP record for this book
is available from the British Library

ISBN 978–0–571–23070–9

10 9 8 7 6 5 4 3 2 1

Contents

Introduction

1

Alexander Pope seemed to come from nowhere. His father was a Roman Catholic, harassed for a faith found to be dynastically threatening: having been forced to move his linen draper's business from Lombard Street, he eventually moved his family out to Binfield, in Windsor Forest. Somehow, from this unlikely environment, Pope at twelve years old set about mastering the art of writing expertly in the manner of most of the reputable poets of the seventeenth century just as that century came to an end. The child Pope knew instinctively what his ambition required:

> Nor with the Israelites shall I desire
>   Thy heav'nly word by Moses to receive,
> Lest I should die: but Thou who didst inspire
>   Moses himself, speak thou, that I may live.
>   (*Paraphrase on Thomas a Kempis*, 13–6)

This privileged plea for inspiration has a ring of conviction: 'speak thou, that I may live.' He was, like Mozart, an infant prodigy, whose extraordinary talents and confidence acted as an immediate passport to the attention of his kindly elders, men like Wycherley and Congreve, who soon found him disconcertingly eager to correct and rewrite their work.

From this early vantage point Pope was primed to understand the busy literary world that he needed to conquer. He raised the money necessary for an independent life by using his contacts to sell a translation of Homer by subscription, and thereafter prided himself on serving no patron or political party. His *Iliad* from 1715 brought him a reputation that was sealed by the issue of his *Poetical Works* in 1717, all this before he was thirty.

Pope's enemies sometimes referred to him nervously as 'Pope Alexander' in allusion to his pontifical authority and ostracised religion, but if they were daring enough he might easily become 'A. P—E', as though the satirist's stature (four foot six, with a deformation of the spine due to Potts disease) could make him somehow as ignorable as a chattering monkey.

But Pope, though tiny, was handsome. Nor was he ignorable, and he did not leave his enemies alone. He arraigned them superbly from the tower of his moral authority. Flattered in youth, he soon came to feel himself impregnable in wisdom and lofty insight into the sexual, cultural and political follies of the age. In fact (as is usually the case with engaged poetry) this tower's fortifications were deeply dependent upon language and rhetoric. And it had been designed for him by experienced architects, poets like Dryden and Rochester, with solid foundations in a bedrock of the ancients, Virgil, Ovid and above all Horace. This was the Mosaic law of his neo-classical inheritance, and as it turned out he perhaps did not need any more direct inspiration, unless it were to discover how truly to 'live' through 'speaking' for himself. For in Pope's case, more perhaps than for most poets up to his time, his individuality of poetic voice was to be achieved by learning how to talk in verse. His own bequest is to poets like Byron and Auden.

To begin with, however, he could afford simply to enjoy himself, whether with a phallic innuendo about the exciting manifestation of the Goddess Flora in rural Berkshire (see 'Where'er you walk, &c' on p. 4) or a playful descriptive periphrasis from his loved home territory of Windsor Forest (see the huntsman on p. 11, pretending through a brilliant diversionary riddle simply to be observing a storm). He never lost his taste for mildly surrealistic effects of this sort. Pope himself knew that a professional poet should begin with pastorals ('pure description') before moving on to more serious stuff ('sense'). Yet even in his youth he had his eye on an epic (the 4,000 lines of *Alcander*, which he burned) and the crowning achievement of his early career turned out to be the mock-epic *The Rape of the Lock*, the gradually expanding text finalised in his 1717 *Works*, perhaps the most perfect poem he ever wrote, and the longest complete poem that I have included here. The miniature heroic events exquisitely performed on tables (dressing table, coffee table, card table) are the summit of Pope's rich descriptive teasing, invoking Greek armour, Roman feasting and the insubstantial angels of Milton, in a milieu of female vanity and flirtation.

2

The earliest version of the *Rape* was written in a fortnight in 1712 as a means of laughing together two estranged Catholic families after offence was taken at a stolen lock of hair. In its final version, the ostensible message of the poem is that a young woman should seize her chances and not play hard to get, since the life of pleasure will not charm the smallpox or chase old age away (see p. 32). Indeed not: the 'real' Baron had died of smallpox in the year after the first version of the poem, and eighteen members of his family died of it within a period of twenty-seven years.

But the *carpe diem* note is complicated by the subtlety of the sexual politics of the poem. The epic parody requires a furious response from the assaulted Belinda, with all the hysterical resources of the Cave of Spleen, and a retributive mock-battle. And for a while we can almost believe in her sense of outrage. But at the same time Pope makes us see that there is an expediency in Belinda's behaviour ('Oh hadst thou, Cruel! Been content to seize / Hairs less in sight, or any Hairs but these!') which shows what a great mistake it would be to lose her honour without material compensation. The lock of hair comes to seem relatively meaningless, something much desired that mysteriously disappears once you take it, like a woman's virginity. To turn it into a shooting star is an Ovidian trick, but the fame that this metamorphosis supposedly brings belongs more properly to the poem itself, and is a purely literary stardom, whose prophecy has been amply fulfilled.

The poem's multiple moral incongruities suggest that it is only to be expected that Belinda herself will ultimately value virginity no more than pets or jewellery, so long as appearances are maintained. And the Baron himself, like the beaux in Pope's *The Temple of Fame*, seems equally content with mere reputation ('Of unknown Dutchesses leud Tales we tell, / Yet would the World believe us, all were well': see p. 10) though he fits very well with Havelock Ellis's description of the commonest of hair-fetishists, the *coupeur des nattes*, of nervous temperament and bad heredity.

For a time in his youth, Pope himself seemed content to play a similar role in his poems, happy to be thought of as a rake. In the suppressed ending of the 'Epistle to Miss Blount on her leaving the Town, after the Coronation', for example, he describes himself as 'hackney'd in Sin', cheerfully resigned to prostitutes in her absence. He paraded his friendship with the ladies-in-waiting at Court, pretending to praise them for their wit as much as their beauty, while at the same time insinuating an ambivalent moral criticism (see, for example, 'The Court Ballad', p. 48). Many of these poems, such as 'A Farewell to London' (p. 39) are in lyric forms unlike his otherwise habitual couplets, and lend an airy lift to this sometimes awkward pose. The claims he makes to possess sexual power strike us as being as fanciful as his Eloisa's ecstasies of deprivation, imagined orgasm and death, when writing to her emasculated lover, but they have a compensating sense of the ridiculous. To the end of his life Pope continued to write brilliant, if prejudiced, poems about women and the way in which their claims upon life and literature tend to confuse and upset men. I have therefore also included the whole of the late *Sober Advice from Horace* (1734), a poem that promotes a wonderful sense of outrage at the sheer difficulty of the sexual relationship.

3

The Dunciad (1728) leaves the drawing room for the streets of Hanoverian London, where a cultural infiltration is in progress, the wholesale movement of the centre of popular entertainment at Bartholomew Fair to the politer end of town. Its hero is Lewis Theobald, an editor who worried about the commas in Shakespeare but himself wrote pantomimes. The perceived aridity of a new 'Duns' Scotus hailed by all Grub Street as 'King Tibbald' is tantamount to the arrival of a new Dark Age, which *The Dunciad* ominously heralds. The poem is the major exhibit of the 'Works of the Unlearned' elaborately planned by the Scriblerus Club of Swift, Pope, Gay and Arbuthnot. *The Dunciad*

Variorum (1729) intensifies the attack on futile scholarship and incompetent writing with mock-apparatus designed to parallel the mock-heroic procedure of the text and extend the savage comedy to appendices and footnotes. Eventually (by the time of *The Dunciad in Four Books*, 1743) this gloomy cataclysm was to take in its sweep the whole of Whig culture ('a new Saturnian age of Lead') with a new hero, the Laureate Colley Cibber, and a heightened sense of the iron grip of the first Prime Minister Walpole and City money on a country grotesquely mesmerised by dullness and corruption. Extracts cannot do justice to this extensive major work of Pope's, but I have included the Cave of Poverty and Poetry, and Tibbald constructing a pyre of his works from Book I, and one of the Games in Book II, from *The Dunciad Variorum*; and the whole of *The New Dunciad* (i.e. Book IV, first published in 1742).

The first of these extracts reminds us that it is Pope's economic success as a writer that permits him his jibes at the starving denizens of Grub Street, as though the literary market were already in a state of equilibrium. In fact, many writers were in a state of penury because they were out of political favour. A poet not of the first rank, who was not prepared to work for Walpole, had a hard time of it. Even the good ones like Prior were saved from misery by the efforts of literate aristocrats like the Earls of Oxford and Bathurst. But the real implication of the Cave is that poor writers are poor because they are entirely ignorant of what is descriptively appropriate and produce work which is symptomatically chaotic. You don't find flowers in the desert, or fruit in the frozen north, but the dunces do, and thereby create a world in which their Goddess is at home. The extract from Book II, where booksellers see who can pee the highest in a competition to win the novelist Eliza Haywood, betrays another Popean prejudice, not so much against a woman writer but against the scandalous popularity of what was already the major new genre of the century (even Daniel Defoe figured as a Dunce in the poem). Pope is adept at disguising his personal motives: Lewis Theobald had publicly itemised the weaknesses of Pope's own edition of Shakespeare, and therefore inevitably exposed himself to Pope's magnificent revenge. Readers have been sensitive to the bold invidiousness of Pope's prejudices, as though required to reach a judicial impartiality in the matter. Sometimes they can forget that poetry can be energised as much by bile as tenderness, and they can forget, too, that Pope was sensitive to the arguments against *ad hominem* satire, and genuinely wanted to be loved as a decent man trying to maintain the moral and educational standards so comprehensively at risk in *The New Dunciad*.

4

In the 1730s Pope embarked on a comprehensive 'Ethick Work' in the manner of Horace, 'fit for my own country, and for my own time'. Like the grand schemes of most poets, it eventually collapsed into its constituent parts (the *Moral Essays*, the *Imitations of Horace*, the *Essay on Man*, and so on). The philosophical drift of this work is an unexceptionable recognition of the status quo and a civilised moderation between extremes, but its great technical discovery is the epistle, which allows Pope to speak with urbanity (that tone of rational discourse between citizens with a shared interest in the health of the *polis* promoting good-humoured concurrence). In this way he achieved the prayed-for authenticity which all poets need in order to live, and to last. All these poems, whether taking up the carefully balanced procedures of an essay or (like the *Epistle to Bathurst*) the high fulminating tone of a sermon, are epistolary in character. The virtues of the addressees are implicated and their assumed responses are accounted for, the given examples are common knowledge needing no special pleading, the arguments wrily understated and the colloquial tone on the whole amused rather than exasperated. The Horatian manner suited Pope's voice, and Pope in turn fulfilled Dryden's prescription that an imitation should allow the Roman poet to 'speak that kind of English, which he would have spoken had he lived in England, and had written to this age'. The range of subjects in Pope's later satire is enormous, but I have given some prominence to money (in *Bathurst*) and food (in *The Second Satire of the Second Book of Horace Paraphased*).

Both of these poems, together with *Sober Advice from Horace*, are given in their entirety, while as something of an antidote both to high-mindedness and the sometimes remorseless heroic couplet I have also included a fair number of *jeux d'esprit*, including a recipe for soup (containing a sequence of riddles for celery, sorrel, thyme and parsley), a poem in the voice of Pope's bitch Bounce, and an extraordinarily whimsical attack on the pretentiousness of Tom D'Urfey, the balladeer.

The main dialectic of the powerful *Bathurst* is the opposition between avarice and profusion, an illustration of the almost mystical theory of balanced plenitude that Pope had expounded in *The Essay on Man* ('All Nature's diff'rence keeps all Nature's peace', iv. 56). But the effect of Pope's *exempla* is of a panoramic Hogarthian delight in the grotesque mismanagement of everything that money (and its latest elusive manifestation, paper credit) represents. As his argument heats up, he abandons pseudo-nyms and types and engages in a direct onslaught upon the public enemies of the state, men like Denis Bond of the Charitable Corporation, or Sir John Blunt, a director of the South Sea Company. The Charitable Corporation was supposed to make loans to the poor, but Bond was reported to have said: 'Damn the poor, let us go into the City, where we may get Money.' Most of the capital of the corporation was appropriated by its chief warehouse-keeper. Blunt is presented as the pious Calvinist who thinks that the poor are damned for not being successful in the world. The great swindle of the South Sea Bubble is later seen ironically as his noble effort to anticipate the general corruption, in terms like those of the progress of Dullness in *The Dunciad*. Bond, Sutton, Heathcote and Blunt supply here evidence of the general trend, of the perversion of charity into big business, and of business into wholesale robbery. What poets of our day are so ready to take on the fat cats of the City?

Whether slyly allusive or directly detailed, this sort of satirical poetry does raise the question of how much the reader needs to know about its characters to get the picture. A pocket edition of this kind has no space for proper annotation, which in any case quite often simply gets in the way. It is for this reason that

I have removed Pope's own ironical footnotes from *The Dunciad* and everywhere left the plain text to speak for itself, as though just published. Swift understood the difficulty, writing to Pope: 'Twenty miles from London, nobody understands hints, initial letters, or town facts and passages; and in a few years not even those who live in London.' A few centuries further on leaves us no clearer about how much we really need to know. To the reader of this small selection there are two simple answers. The first is the practical solution of chasing up any particular difficulty or interest that may arise by consulting the annotations and apparatus of the six-volume Twickenham Edition of Pope (Methuen and Co.). The second is the perhaps less reliable assurance that Pope's drift is usually perfectly comprehensible with a dictionary and that a historical person, whether fully named or not, is always contextually alive, becoming the appropriate victim by virtue of the evidence of the poem and not of that person's life. Pope constructed wonderful and elaborate arguments to show that 'the Poem was not made for these Authors, but these Authors for the Poem'. The absurd extreme of such an argument throws justice and biography to the winds: 'Had the Hero [of *The Dunciad*], for instance, been called *Codrus*, how many would have affirmed him to be Mr W—, Mr D—, Sir R— B—, Etc. but now all that unjust scandal is saved, by calling him *Theobald*, which by good luck happens to be the name of a real person.'

It is our good luck that at this moment in the early eighteenth century, when the modern world of newspapers, novels, global enterprise, utilitarian justification of economic exploitation, popular entertainment and blinkered scientific research was just lurching into being, there should arise a poet of genius who could give it all a long hard stare in a stubborn but delighted mood of Horatian *nil admirari* ('don't be fooled for a moment'). Pope supremely discovered how to give aesthetic life to processes of thought, and like many writers who were outsiders in their day, resistant to the dominant energies, he woos us with both ferocity and detachment.

JOHN FULLER

ALEXANDER POPE

Artemisia

Tho' *Artimesia* talks, by Fits,
Of Councils, Classicks, Fathers, Wits;
   Reads *Malbranche, Boyle*, and *Locke*:
Yet in some Things methinks she fails,
'Twere well if she would pare her Nails,
   And wear a cleaner Smock.

Haughty and huge as *High-Dutch* Bride,
Such Nastiness and so much Pride
   Are odly join'd by Fate:
On her large Squab you find her spread,
Like a fat Corpse upon a Bed,
   That lies and stinks in State.

She wears no Colours (sign of Grace)
On any Part except her Face;
   All white and black beside:
Dauntless her Look, her Gesture proud,
Her Voice theatrically loud,
   And masculine her Stride.

So have I seen, in black and white
A prating Thing, a Magpy height,
   Majestically stalk;
A stately, worthless Animal,
That plies the Tongue, and wags the Tail,
   All Flutter, Pride, and Talk.

from Pastorals: Summer

[*lines 59–92*]

See what Delights in Sylvan Scenes appear!
Descending Gods have found *Elysium* here.
In Woods bright *Venus* with *Adonis* stray'd,
And chast *Diana* haunts the Forest Shade.
Come lovely Nymph, and bless the silent Hours,
When Swains from Sheering seek their nightly
    Bow'rs;
When weary Reapers quit the sultry Field,
And crown'd with Corn, their Thanks to *Ceres* yield.
This harmless Grove no lurking Viper hides,
But in my Breast the Serpent Love abides.
Here Bees from Blossoms sip the rosie Dew,
But your *Alexis* knows no Sweets but you.
Oh deign to visit our forsaken Seats,
The mossie Fountains, and the Green Retreats!
Where-e'er you walk, cool Gales shall fan the Glade,
Trees, where you sit, shall crowd into a Shade,
Where-e'er you tread, the blushing Flow'rs shall rise,
And all things flourish where you turn your Eyes.
Oh! how I long with you to pass my Days,
Invoke the Muses, and resound your Praise;
Your Praise the Birds shall chant in ev'ry Grove,
And Winds shall waft it to the Pow'rs above.
But wou'd you sing, and rival *Orpheus*' Strain,
The wondring Forests soon shou'd dance again,
The moving Mountains hear the pow'rful Call,
And headlong Streams hang list'ning in their Fall!

But see, the Shepherds shun the Noon-day Heat,
The lowing Herds to murm'ring Brooks retreat,
To closer Shades the panting Flocks remove,
Ye Gods! and is there no Relief for Love?

But soon the Sun with milder Rays descends
To the cool Ocean, where his Journey ends;
On me Love's fiercer Flames for ever prey,
By Night he scorches, as he burns by Day.

from An Essay on Criticism,
   [*lines 337–73*]

But most by *Numbers* judge a Poet's Song,
And *smooth* or *rough*, with them, is *right* or *wrong*;
In the bright *Muse* tho' thousand *Charms* conspire,
Her *Voice* is all these tuneful Fools admire,
Who haunt *Parnassus* but to please their Ear,
Not mend their Minds; as some to *Church* repair,
Not for the *Doctrine*, but the *Musick* there.
These *Equal Syllables* alone require,
Tho' oft the Ear the *open Vowels* tire,
While *Expletives* their feeble Aid *do* join,
And ten low Words oft creep in one dull Line,
While they ring round the same *unvary'd Chimes*,
With sure *Returns* of still *expected Rhymes*.
Where-e'er you find *the cooling Western Breeze*,
In the next Line, it *whispers thro' the Trees*;
If *Chrystal Streams with pleasing Murmurs creep*,
The Reader's threaten'd (not in vain) with *Sleep*.
Then, at the *last*, and *only* Couplet fraught
With some *unmeaning* Thing they call a *Thought*,
A *needless Alexandrine* ends the Song,
That like a wounded Snake, drags its slow length along.
Leave such to tune their own dull Rhimes, and know
What's *roundly smooth*, or *languishingly slow*;
And praise the *Easie Vigor* of a Line,
Where *Denham*'s Strength, and *Waller*'s Sweetness join.
True Ease in Writing comes from Art, not Chance,
As those move easiest who have learn'd to dance.
'Tis not enough no Harshness gives Offence,
The *Sound* must seem an *Eccho* to the *Sense*.
Soft is the Strain when *Zephyr* gently blows,
And the *smooth Stream* in *smoother Numbers* flows;
But when loud Surges lash the sounding Shore,

The *hoarse, rough Verse* shou'd like the *Torrent* roar.
When *Ajax* strives, some Rocks' vast Weight to throw,
The Line too *labours*, and the Words move *slow*;
Not so, when swift *Camilla* scours the Plain,
Flies o'er th'unbending Corn, and skims along the Main.

from Epistle to Miss Blount, With the Works
   of Voiture
   [*lines 49–68*]

The Gods, to curse *Pamela* with her Pray'rs,
Gave the gilt Coach and dappled *Flanders* Mares,
The shining Robes, rich Jewels, Beds of State,
And to compleat her Bliss, a Fool for Mate.
She glares in *Balls, Front-boxes*, and the *Ring*,
A vain, unquiet, glitt'ring, wretched Thing!
Pride, Pomp, and State but reach her outward Part,
She sighs, and is no *Dutchess* at her Heart.
   But, Madam, if the Fates withstand, and you
Are destin'd *Hymen*'s willing Victim too,
Trust not too much your now resistless Charms,
Those, Age or Sickness, soon or late, disarms;
Good Humour only teaches Charms to last,
Still makes new Conquests, and maintains the past:
Love, rais'd on Beauty, will like That decay,
Our Hearts may bear its slender Chain a Day,
As flow'ry Bands in Wantonness are worn;
A Morning's Pleasure, and at Evening torn:
This binds in Ties more easie, yet more strong,
The willing Heart, and only holds it long.

from The Temple of Fame
[*lines 356–91*]

    Then came the smallest Tribe I yet had seen,
Plain was their Dress, and modest was their Mein.
Great Idol of Mankind! we neither claim
The Praise of Merit, nor aspire to Fame;
But safe in Desarts from th' Applause of Men,
Would die unheard of, as we liv'd unseen.
'Tis all we beg thee, to conceal from Sight
Those Acts of Goodness, which themselves requite.
O let us still the secret Joy partake,
To follow Virtue ev'n for Virtue's sake.

    And live there Men who slight immortal Fame?
Who then with Incense shall adore our Name?
But Mortals! know, 'tis still our greatest Pride,
To blaze those Virtues which the Good would hide.
Rise! Muses, rise! add all your tuneful Breath,
These must not sleep in Darkness and in Death.
She said: in Air the trembling Musick floats,
And on the Winds triumphant swell the Notes;
So soft, tho high, so loud, and yet so clear,
Ev'n list'ning Angels lean'd from Heaven to hear:
To farthest Shores th' Ambrosial Spirit flies,
Sweet to the World, and grateful to the Skies.

    Next these a youthful Train their Vows exprest,
With Feathers crown'd, with gay Embroid'ry drest;
Hither, they cry'd, direct your Eyes, and see
The Men of Pleasure, Dress, and Gallantry:
Ours is the Place at Banquets, Balls and Plays;
Sprightly our Nights, polite are all our Days;
Courts we frequent, where 'tis our pleasing Care
To pay due Visits, and address the Fair:
In fact, 'tis true, no Nymph we cou'd persuade,
But still in Fancy vanquish'd ev'ry Maid;

Of unknown Dutchesses leud Tales we tell,
Yet would the World believe us, all were well.
The Joy let others have, and we the Name,
And what we want in Pleasure, grant in Fame.

from Windsor-Forest

[*lines 111–34 and 327–54*]

See! from the Brake the whirring Pheasant springs,
And mounts exulting on triumphant Wings;
Short is his Joy! he feels the fiery Wound,
Flutters in Blood, and panting beats the Ground.
Ah! what avail his glossie, varying Dyes,
His Purple Crest, and Scarlet-circled Eyes,
The vivid Green his shining Plumes unfold;
His painted Wings, and Breast that flames with Gold?
    Nor yet, when moist *Arcturus* clouds the Sky,
The Woods and Fields their pleasing Toils deny.
To Plains with well-breath'd Beagles we repair,
And trace the Mazes of the circling Hare.
(Beasts, urg'd by us, their Fellow Beasts pursue,
And learn of Man each other to undo.)
With slaught'ring Guns th'unweary'd Fowler roves,
When Frosts have whiten'd all the naked Groves;
Where Doves in Flocks the leafless Trees o'ershade,
And lonely Woodcocks haunt the watry Glade.
He lifts the Tube, and levels with his Eye;
Strait a short Thunder breaks the frozen Sky.
Oft, as in Airy Rings they skim the Heath,
The clam'rous Lapwings feel the Leaden Death:
Oft as the mounting Larks their Notes prepare,
They fall, and leave their little Lives in Air.

*

At length great *ANNA* said – Let Discord cease!
She said, the World obey'd, and all was *Peace*!
    In that blest Moment, from his Oozy Bed
Old Father *Thames* advanc'd his rev'rend Head.
His Tresses dropt with Dews, and o'er the Stream
His shining Horns diffus'd a golden Gleam:

Grav'd on his Urn appear'd the Moon, that guides
His swelling Waters, and alternate Tydes;
The figur'd Streams in Waves of Silver roll'd,
And on their Banks *Augusta* rose in Gold.
Around his Throne the Sea-born Brothers stood,
Who swell with Tributary Urns his Flood.
First the fam'd Authors of his ancient Name,
The winding *Isis*, and the fruitful *Tame*:
The *Kennet* swift, for silver Eels renown'd;
The *Loddon* slow, with verdant Alders crown'd:
Cole, whose dark Streams his flow'ry Islands lave;
And chalky *Wey*, that rolls a milky Wave:
The blue, transparent *Vandalis* appears;
The gulphy *Lee* his sedgy Tresses rears:
And sullen *Mole*, that hides his diving Flood;
And silent *Darent*, stain'd with *Danish* Blood.

　　High in the midst, upon his Urn reclin'd,
(His Sea-green Mantle waving with the Wind)
The God appear'd; he turn'd his azure Eyes
Where *Windsor*-Domes and pompous Turrets rise,
Then bow'd and spoke; the Winds forget to roar,
And the hush'd Waves glide softly to the Shore.

from To Mr Addison, Occasioned by his Dialogues on Medals
[*lines 1–30*]

See the wild Waste of all-devouring years!
How Rome her own sad Sepulchre appears,
With nodding arches, broken temples spread!
The very Tombs now vanish'd like their dead!
Imperial wonders rais'd on Nations spoil'd,
Where mix'd with Slaves the groaning Martyr toil'd;
Huge Theatres, that now unpeopled Woods,
Now drain'd a distant country of her Floods;
Fanes, which admiring Gods with pride survey,
Statues of Men, scarce less alive than they;
Some felt the silent stroke of mould'ring age,
Some hostile fury, some religious rage;
Barbarian blindness, Christian zeal conspire,
And Papal piety, and Gothic fire.
Perhaps, by its own ruins sav'd from flame,
Some bury'd marble half preserves a name;
That Name the learn'd with fierce disputes pursue,
And give to Titus old Vespasian's due.
   Ambition sigh'd; She found it vain to trust
The faithless Column and the crumbling Bust;
Huge moles, whose shadow stretch'd from shore to shore,
Their ruins ruin'd, and their place no more!
Convinc'd, she now contracts her vast design,
And all her Triumphs shrink into a Coin:
A narrow orb each crouded conquest keeps,
Beneath her Palm here sad Judæa weeps,
Here scantier limits the proud Arch confine,
And scarce are seen the prostrate Nile or Rhine,
A small Euphrates thro' the piece is roll'd,
And little Eagles wave their wings in gold.

The Rape of The Lock

What dire Offence from am'rous Causes springs,
What mighty Contests rise from trivial Things,
I sing – This Verse to *Caryll*, Muse! is due;
This, ev'n *Belinda* may vouchsafe to view:
Slight is the Subject, but not so the Praise,
If She inspire, and He approve my Lays.

Say what strange Motive, Goddess! cou'd compel
A well-bred *Lord* t'assault a gentle *Belle*?
Oh say what stranger Cause, yet unexplor'd,
Cou'd make a gentle *Belle* reject a *Lord*?
In Tasks so bold, can Little Men engage,
And in soft Bosoms dwells such mighty Rage?

Sol thro' white Curtains shot a tim'rous Ray,
And op'd those Eyes that must eclipse the Day;
Now Lapdogs give themselves the rowzing Shake,
And sleepless Lovers, just at Twelve, awake:
Thrice rung the Bell, the Slipper knock'd the Ground,
And the press'd Watch return'd a silver Sound.
Belinda still her downy Pillow prest,
Her Guardian *Sylph* prolong'd the balmy Rest.
'Twas he had summon'd to her silent Bed
The Morning-Dream that hover'd o'er her Head.
A Youth more glitt'ring than a *Birth-night Beau*,
(That ev'n in Slumber caus'd her Cheek to glow)
Seem'd to her Ear his winning Lips to lay,
And thus in Whispers said, or seem'd to say.

Fairest of Mortals, thou distinguish'd Care
Of thousand bright Inhabitants of Air!
If e'er one Vision touch'd thy infant Thought,
Of all the Nurse and all the Priest have taught,
Of airy Elves by Moonlight Shadows seen,

The silver Token, and the circled Green,
Or Virgins visited by Angel-Pow'rs,
With Golden Crowns and Wreaths of heavn'ly Flow'rs,
Hear and believe! thy own Importance know,
Nor bound thy narrow Views to Things below.
Some secret Truths from Learned Pride conceal'd,
To Maids alone and Children are reveal'd:
What tho' no Credit doubting Wits may give?
The Fair and Innocent shall still believe.
Know then, unnumber'd Spirits round thee fly,
The light *Militia* of the lower Sky;
These, tho' unseen, are ever on the Wing,
Hang o'er the *Box*, and hover round the *Ring*.
Think what an Equipage thou hast in Air,
And view with scorn *Two Pages* and a *Chair*.
As now your own, our Beings were of old,
And once inclos'd in Woman's beauteous Mold;
Thence, by a soft Transition, we repair
From earthly Vehicles to these of Air.
Think not, when Woman's transient Breath is fled,
That all her Vanities at once are dead:
Succeeding Vanities she still regards,
And tho' she plays no more, o'erlooks the Cards.
Her Joy in gilded Chariots, when alive,
And Love of *Ombre*, after Death survive.
For when the Fair in all their Pride expire,
To their first Elements their Souls retire:
The Sprights of fiery Termagants in Flame
Mount up, and take a *Salamander*'s Name.
Soft yielding Minds to Water glide away,
And sip with *Nymphs*, their Elemental Tea.
The graver Prude sinks downward to a *Gnome*,
In search of Mischief still on Earth to roam.
The light Coquettes in *Sylphs* aloft repair,
And sport and flutter in the Fields of Air.

Know farther yet; Whoever fair and chaste
Rejects Mankind, is by some *Sylph* embrac'd:
For Spirits, freed from mortal Laws, with ease
Assume what Sexes and what Shapes they please.
What guards the Purity of melting Maids,
In Courtly Balls, and Midnight Masquerades,
Safe from the treach'rous Friend, the daring Spark,
The Glance by Day, the Whisper in the Dark;
When kind Occasion prompts their warm Desires,
When Musick softens, and when Dancing fires?
'Tis but their *Sylph*, the wise Celestials know,
Tho '*Honour* is the Word with Men below.
   Some Nymphs there are, too conscious of their Face,
For Life predestin'd to the *Gnomes*' Embrace.
These swell their Prospects and exalt their Pride,
When Offers are disdain'd, and Love deny'd.
Then gay Ideas crowd the vacant Brain;
While Peers and Dukes, and all their sweeping Train,
And Garters, Stars and Coronets appear,
And in soft Sounds, *Your Grace* salutes their Ear.
'Tis these that early taint the Female Soul,
Instruct the Eyes of young *Coquettes* to roll,
Teach Infant-Cheeks a bidden Blush to know,
And little Hearts to flutter at a *Beau*.
   Oft when the World imagine Women stray,
The *Sylphs* thro' mystick Mazes guide their Way,
Thro' all the giddy Circle they pursue,
And old Impertinence expel by new.
What tender Maid but must a Victim fall
To one Man's Treat, but for another's Ball?
When *Florio* speaks, what Virgin could withstand,
If gentle *Damon* did not squeeze her Hand?
With varying Vanities, from ev'ry Part,
They shift the moving Toyshop of their Heart;
Where Wigs with Wigs, with Sword-knots Sword-knots strive,
Beaus banish Beaus, and Coaches Coaches drive.

This erring Mortals Levity may call,
Oh blind to Truth! the *Sylphs* contrive it all.

Of these am I, who thy Protection claim,
A watchful Sprite, and *Ariel* is my Name.
Late, as I rang'd the Crystal Wilds of Air,
In the clear Mirror of thy ruling *Star*
I saw, alas! some dread Event impend,
Ere to the Main this Morning Sun descend.
But Heav'n reveals not what, or how, or where:
Warn'd by thy *Sylph*, oh Pious Maid beware!
This to disclose is all thy Guardian can.
Beware of all, but most beware of Man!

He said; when *Shock*, who thought she slept too long,
Leapt up, and wak'd his Mistress with his Tongue.
'Twas then *Belinda*! if Report say true,
Thy Eyes first open'd on a *Billet-doux*;
Wounds, Charms, and *Ardors*, were no sooner read,
But all the Vision vanish'd from thy Head.

And now, unveil'd, the *Toilet* stands display'd,
Each Silver Vase in mystic Order laid.
First, rob'd in White, the Nymph intent adores
With Head uncover'd, the *Cosmetic* Pow'rs.
A heav'nly Image in the Glass appears,
To that she bends, to that her Eyes she rears;
Th'inferior Priestess, at her Altar's side,
Trembling, begins the sacred Rites of Pride.
Unnumber'd Treasures ope at once, and here
The various Off'rings of the World appear;
From each she nicely culls with curious Toil,
And decks the Goddess with the glitt'ring Spoil.
This Casket *India*'s glowing Gems unlocks,
And all *Arabia* breathes from yonder Box.
The Tortoise here and Elephant unite,
Transform'd to *Combs*, the speckled and the white.
Here Files of Pins extend their shining Rows,
Puffs, Powders, Patches, Bibles, Billet-doux.

Now awful Beauty puts on all its Arms;
The Fair each moment rises in her Charms,
Repairs her Smiles, awakens ev'ry Grace,
And calls forth all the Wonders of her Face;
Sees by Degrees a purer Blush arise,
And keener Lightnings quicken in her Eyes.
The busy *Sylphs* surround their darling Care;
These set the Head, and those divide the Hair,
Some fold the Sleeve, whilst others plait the Gown;
And *Betty's* prais'd for Labours not her own.

CANTO II

Not with more Glories, in th' Etherial Plain,
The Sun first rises o'er the purpled Main,
Than issuing forth, the Rival of his Beams
Lanch'd on the Bosom of the Silver *Thames*.
Fair Nymphs, and well-drest Youths around her shone,
But ev'ry Eye was fix'd on her alone.
On her white Breast a sparkling *Cross* she wore,
Which *Jews* might kiss, and Infidels adore.
Her lively Looks a sprightly Mind disclose,
Quick as her Eyes, and as unfix'd as those:
Favours to none, to all she Smiles extends,
Oft she rejects, but never once offends.
Bright as the Sun, her Eyes the Gazers strike,
And, like the Sun, they shine on all alike.
Yet graceful Ease, and Sweetness void of Pride,
Might hide her Faults, if *Belles* had Faults to hide:
If to her share some Female Errors fall,
Look on her Face, and you'll forget 'em all.

    This Nymph, to the Destruction of Mankind,
Nourish'd two Locks, which graceful hung behind
In equal Curls, and well conspir'd to deck
With shining Ringlets the smooth Iv'ry Neck.
Love in these Labyrinths his Slaves detains,

And mighty Hearts are held in slender Chains.
With hairy Sprindges we the Birds betray,
Slight Lines of Hair surprize the Finny Prey,
Fair Tresses Man's Imperial Race insnare,
And Beauty draws us with a single Hair.

Th' Adventrous *Baron* the bright Locks admir'd,
He saw, he wish'd, and to the Prize aspir'd:
Resolv'd to win, he meditates the way,
By Force to ravish, or by Fraud betray;
For when Success a Lover's Toil attends,
Few ask, if Fraud or Force attain'd his Ends.

For this, ere *Phœbus* rose, he had implor'd
Propitious Heav'n, and ev'ry Pow'r ador'd,
But chiefly *Love* – to *Love* an Altar built,
Of twelve vast *French* Romances, neatly gilt.
There lay three Garters, half a Pair of Gloves;
And all the Trophies of his former Loves.
With tender *Billet-doux* he lights the Pyre,
And breathes three am'rous Sighs to raise the Fire.
Then prostrate falls, and begs with ardent Eyes
Soon to obtain, and long possess the Prize:
The Pow'rs gave Ear, and granted half his Pray'r,
The rest, the Winds dispers'd in empty Air.

But now secure the painted Vessel glides,
The Sun-beams trembling on the floating Tydes,
While melting Musick steals upon the Sky,
And soften'd Sounds along the Waters die.
Smooth flow the Waves, the Zephyrs gently play,
Belinda smil'd, and all the World was gay.
All but the *Sylph* – With careful Thoughts opprest,
Th'impending Woe sate heavy on his Breast.
He summons strait his Denizens of Air;
The lucid Squadrons round the Sails repair:
Soft o'er the Shrouds Aerial Whispers breathe,
That seem'd but *Zephyrs* to the Train beneath.
Some to the Sun their Insect-Wings unfold,

Waft on the Breeze, or sink in Clouds of Gold.
Transparent Forms, too fine for mortal Sight,
Their fluid Bodies half dissolv'd in Light.
Loose to the Wind their airy Garments flew,
Thin glitt'ring Textures of the filmy Dew;
Dipt in the richest Tincture of the Skies,
Where Light disports in ever-mingling Dies,
While ev'ry Beam new transient Colours flings,
Colours that change whene'er they wave their Wings.
Amid the Circle, on the gilded Mast,
Superior by the Head, was *Ariel* plac'd;
His Purple Pinions opening to the Sun,
He rais'd his Azure Wand, and thus begun.

Ye *Sylphs* and *Sylphids*, to your Chief give Ear,
Fays, Fairies, Genii, Elves, and *Dæmons* hear!
Ye know the Spheres and various Tasks assign'd,
By Laws Eternal, to th' Aerial Kind.
Some in the Fields of purest *Æther* play,
And bask and whiten in the Blaze of Day.
Some guide the Course of wandring Orbs on high,
Or roll the Planets thro' the boundless Sky.
Some less refin'd, beneath the Moon's pale Light
Pursue the Stars that shoot athwart the Night,
Or suck the Mists in grosser Air below,
Or dip their Pinions in the painted Bow,
Or brew fierce Tempests on the wintry Main,
Or o'er the Glebe distill the kindly Rain.
Others on Earth o'er human Race preside,
Watch all their Ways, and all their Actions guide:
Of these the Chief the Care of Nations own,
And guard with Arms Divine the *British Throne*.

Our humbler Province is to tend the Fair,
Not a less pleasing, tho' less glorious Care.
To save the Powder from too rude a Gale,
Nor let th' imprison'd Essences exhale,
To draw fresh Colours from the vernal Flow'rs,

To steal from Rainbows ere they drop in Show'rs
A brighter Wash; to curl their waving Hairs,
Assist their Blushes, and inspire their Airs;
Nay oft, in Dreams, Invention we bestow,
To change a *Flounce*, or add a *Furbelo*.

This Day, black Omens threat the brightest Fair
That e'er deserv'd a watchful Spirit's Care;
Some dire Disaster, or by Force, or Slight,
But what, or where, the Fates have wrapt in Night.
Whether the Nymph shall break *Diana*'s Law,
Or some frail *China* Jar receive a Flaw,
Or stain her Honour, or her new Brocade,
Forget her Pray'rs, or miss a Masquerade,
Or lose her Heart, or Necklace, at a Ball;
Or whether Heav'n has doom'd that *Shock* must fall.
Haste then ye Spirits! to your Charge repair;
The flutt'ring Fan be *Zephyretta*'s Care;
The Drops to thee, *Brillante*, we consign;
And, *Momentilla*, let the Watch be thine;
Do thou, *Crispissa*, tend her fav'rite Lock;
Ariel himself shall be the Guard of *Shock*.

To Fifty chosen *Sylphs*, of special Note,
We trust th' important Charge, the *Petticoat*:
Oft have we known that sev'nfold Fence to fail,
Tho' stiff with Hoops, and arm'd with Ribs of Whale.
Form a strong Line about the Silver Bound,
And guard the wide Circumference around.

Whatever Spirit, careless of his Charge,
His Post neglects, or leaves the Fair at large,
Shall feel sharp Vengeance soon o'ertake his Sins,
Be stopt in *Vials*, or transfixt with *Pins*;
Or plung'd in Lakes of bitter *Washes* lie,
Or wedg'd whole Ages in a *Bodkin*'s Eye:
Gums and *Pomatums* shall his Flight restrain,
While clog'd he beats his silken Wings in vain;
Or Alom-*Stypticks* with contracting Power

Shrink his thin Essence like a rivell'd Flower.
Or as *Ixion* fix'd, the Wretch shall feel
The giddy Motion of the whirling Mill,
In Fumes of burning Chocolate shall glow,
And tremble at the Sea that froaths below!

He spoke; the Spirits from the Sails descend;
Some, Orb in Orb, around the Nymph extend,
Some thrid the mazy Ringlets of her Hair,
Some hang upon the Pendants of her Ear;
With beating Hearts the dire Event they wait,
Anxious, and trembling for the Birth of Fate.

CANTO III

Close by those Meads for ever crown'd with Flow'rs,
Where *Thames* with Pride surveys his rising Tow'rs,
There stands a Structure of Majestick Frame,
Which from the neighb'ring *Hampton* takes its Name.
Here *Britain*'s Statesmen oft the Fall foredoom
Of Foreign Tyrants, and of Nymphs at home;
Here Thou, Great *Anna*! whom three Realms obey,
Dost sometimes Counsel take – and sometimes *Tea*.

Hither the Heroes and the Nymphs resort,
To taste awhile the Pleasures of a Court;
In various Talk th' instructive hours they past,
Who gave the *Ball*, or paid the *Visit* last:
One speaks the Glory of the *British Queen*,
And one describes a charming *Indian Screen*;
A third interprets Motions, Looks, and Eyes;
At ev'ry Word a Reputation dies.
Snuff, or the *Fan*, supply each Pause of Chat,
With singing, laughing, ogling, and all that.

Mean while declining from the Noon of Day,
The Sun obliquely shoots his burning Ray;
The hungry Judges soon the Sentence sign,
And Wretches hang that Jury-men may Dine;

The Merchant from th' *Exchange* returns in Peace,
And the long Labours of the *Toilette* cease–
Belinda now, whom Thirst of Fame invites,
Burns to encounter two adventrous Knights,
At *Ombre* singly to decide their Doom;
And swells her Breast with Conquests yet to come.
Strait the three Bands prepare in Arms to join,
Each Band the number of the Sacred Nine.
Soon as she spreads her Hand, th' Aerial Guard
Descend, and sit on each important Card:
First *Ariel* perch'd upon a *Matadore*,
Then each, according to the Rank they bore;
For *Sylphs*, yet mindful of their ancient Race,
Are, as when Women, wondrous fond of Place.

   Behold, four *Kings* in Majesty rever'd,
With hoary Whiskers and a forky Beard;
And four fair *Queens* whose hands sustain a Flow'r,
Th' expressive Emblem of their softer Pow'r;
Four *Knaves* in Garbs succinct, a trusty Band,
Caps on their heads, and Halberds in their hand;
And Particolour'd Troops, a shining Train,
Draw forth to Combat on the Velvet Plain.

   The skilful Nymph reviews her Force with Care;
Let Spades be Trumps! she said, and Trumps they were.

   Now move to War her Sable *Matadores*,
In Show like Leaders of the swarthy *Moors*.
Spadillio first, unconquerable Lord!
Led off two captive Trumps, and swept the Board.
As many more *Manillio* forc'd to yield,
And march'd a Victor from the verdant Field.
Him *Basto* follow'd, but his Fate more hard
Gain'd but one Trump and one *Plebeian* Card.
With his broad Sabre next, a Chief in Years,
The hoary Majesty of *Spades* appears;
Puts forth one manly Leg, to sight reveal'd;
The rest his many-colour'd Robe conceal'd.

The Rebel-*Knave*, who dares his Prince engage,
Proves the just Victim of his Royal Rage.
Ev'n mighty *Pam* that Kings and Queens o'erthrew,
And mow'd down Armies in the Fights of *Lu*,
Sad Chance of War! now, destitute of Aid,
Falls undistinguish'd by the Victor *Spade*!

Thus far both Armies to *Belinda* yield;
Now to the *Baron* Fate inclines the Field.
His warlike *Amazon* her Host invades,
Th' Imperial Consort of the Crown of *Spades*.
The *Club*'s black Tyrant first her Victim dy'd,
Spite of his haughty Mien, and barb'rous Pride:
What boots the Regal Circle on his Head,
His Giant Limbs in State unwieldy spread?
That long behind he trails his pompous Robe,
And of all Monarchs only grasps the Globe?

The *Baron* now his *Diamonds* pours apace;
Th' embroider'd *King* who shows but half his Face,
And his refulgent *Queen*, with Pow'rs combin'd,
Of broken Troops an easie Conquest find.
Clubs, Diamonds, Hearts, in wild Disorder seen,
With Throngs promiscuous strow the level Green.
Thus when dispers'd a routed Army runs,
Of *Asia*'s Troops, and *Africk*'s Sable Sons,
With like Confusion different Nations fly,
Of various Habit and of various Dye,
The pierc'd Battalions dis-united fall,
In Heaps on Heaps; one Fate o'erwhelms them all.

The *Knave of Diamonds* tries his wily Arts,
And wins (oh shameful Chance!) the *Queen of Hearts*.
At this, the Blood the Virgin's Cheek forsook,
A livid Paleness spreads o'er all her Look;
She sees, and trembles at th' approaching Ill,
Just in the Jaws of Ruin, and *Codille*.
And now, (as oft in some distemper'd State)
On one nice *Trick* depends the gen'ral Fate.

An *Ace* of Hearts steps forth: The *King* unseen
Lurk'd in her Hand, and mourn'd his captive *Queen*.
He springs to Vengeance with an eager pace,
And falls like Thunder on the prostrate *Ace*.
The Nymph exulting fills with Shouts the Sky,
The Walls, the Woods, and long Canals reply.

   Oh thoughtless Mortals! ever blind to Fate,
Too soon dejected, and too soon elate!
Sudden these Honours shall be snatch'd away,
And curs'd for ever this Victorious Day,

   For lo! the Board with Cups and Spoons is crown'd,
The Berries crackle, and the Mill turns round.
On shining Altars of *Japan* they raise
The silver Lamp; the fiery Spirits blaze.
From silver Spouts the grateful Liquors glide,
While *China*'s Earth receives the smoking Tyde.
At once they gratify their Scent and Taste,
And frequent Cups prolong the rich Repast.
Strait hover round the Fair her Airy Band;
Some, as she sip'd, the fuming Liquor fann'd,
Some o'er her Lap their careful Plumes display'd,
Trembling, and conscious of the rich Brocade.
Coffee, (which makes the Politician wise,
And see thro' all things with his half-shut Eyes)
Sent up in Vapours to the *Baron*'s Brain
New Stratagems, the radiant Lock to gain.
Ah cease rash Youth! desist ere 'tis too late,
Fear the just Gods, and think of *Scylla*'s Fate!
Chang'd to a Bird, and sent to flit in Air,
She dearly pays for *Nisus*' injur'd Hair!

   But when to Mischief Mortals bend their Will,
How soon they find fit Instruments of Ill!
Just then, *Clarissa* drew with tempting Grace
A two-edg'd Weapon from her shining Case;
So Ladies in Romance assist their Knight,
Present the Spear, and arm him for the Fight.

He takes the Gift with rev'rence, and extends
The little Engine on his Fingers' Ends,
This just behind *Belinda*'s Neck he spread,
As o'er the fragrant Steams she bends her Head:
Swift to the Lock a thousand Sprights repair,
A thousand Wings, by turns, blow back the Hair,
And thrice they twitch'd the Diamond in her Ear,
Thrice she look'd back, and thrice the Foe drew near.
Just in that instant, anxious *Ariel* sought
The close Recesses of the Virgin's Thought;
As on the Nosegay in her Breast reclin'd,
He watch'd th' Ideas rising in her Mind,
Sudden he view'd, in spite of all her Art,
An Earthly Lover lurking at her Heart.
Amaz'd, confus'd, he found his Pow'r expir'd,
Resign'd to Fate, and with a Sigh retir'd.

   The Peer now spreads the glitt'ring *Forfex* wide,
T'inclose the Lock; now joins it, to divide.
Ev'n then, before the fatal Engine clos'd,
A wretched *Sylph* too fondly interpos'd;
Fate urg'd the Sheers, and cut the *Sylph* in twain,
(But Airy Substance soon unites again)
The meeting Points the sacred Hair dissever
From the fair Head, for ever and for ever!

   Then flash'd the living Lightning from her Eyes,
And Screams of Horror rend th' affrighted Skies.
Not louder Shrieks to pitying Heav'n are cast,
When Husbands or when Lap-dogs breathe their last,
Or when rich *China* Vessels, fal'n from high,
In glittring Dust and painted Fragments lie!

   Let Wreaths of Triumph now my Temples twine,
(The Victor cry'd) the glorious Prize is mine!
While Fish in Streams, or Birds delight in Air,
Or in a Coach and Six the *British* Fair,
As long as *Atalantis* shall be read,
Or the small Pillow grace a Lady's Bed,

While *Visits* shall be paid on solemn Days,
When numerous Wax-lights in bright Order blaze,
While Nymphs take Treats, or Assignations give,
So long my Honour, Name, and Praise shall live!

What Time wou'd spare, from Steel receives its date,
And Monuments, like Men, submit to Fate!
Steel cou'd the Labour of the Gods destroy,
And strike to Dust th' Imperial Tow'rs of *Troy*;
Steel cou'd the Works of mortal Pride confound,
And hew Triumphal Arches to the Ground.
What Wonder then, fair Nymph! thy Hairs shou'd feel
The conqu'ring Force of unresisted Steel?

CANTO IV

But anxious Cares the pensive Nymph opprest,
And secret Passions labour'd in her Breast.
Not youthful Kings in Battel seiz'd alive,
Not scornful Virgins who their Charms survive,
Not ardent Lovers robb'd of all their Bliss,
Not ancient Ladies when refus'd a Kiss,
Not Tyrants fierce that unrepenting die,
Not *Cynthia* when her *Manteau*'s pinn'd awry,
E'er felt such Rage, Resentment and Despair,
As Thou, sad Virgin! for thy ravish'd Hair.

For, that sad moment, when the *Sylphs* withdrew,
And *Ariel* weeping from *Belinda* flew,
Umbriel, a dusky melancholy Spright,
As ever sully'd the fair face of Light,
Down to the Central Earth, his proper Scene,
Repair'd to search the gloomy Cave of *Spleen*.

Swift on his sooty Pinions flitts the *Gnome*,
And in a Vapour reach'd the dismal Dome.
No cheerful Breeze this sullen Region knows,
The dreaded *East* is all the Wind that blows.
Here, in a Grotto, sheltred close from Air,

And screen'd in Shades from Day's detested Glare,
She sighs for ever on her pensive Bed,
Pain at her Side, and *Megrim* at her Head.

Two Handmaids wait the Throne: Alike in Place,
But diff'ring far in Figure and in Face.
Here stood *Ill-nature* like an *ancient Maid*,
Her wrinkled Form in *Black* and *White* array'd;
With store of Pray'rs, for Mornings, Nights, and Noons,
Her Hand is fill'd; her Bosom with Lampoons.

There *Affectation* with a sickly Mien
Shows in her Cheek the Roses of Eighteen,
Practis'd to Lisp, and hang the Head aside,
Faints into Airs, and languishes with Pride;
On the rich Quilt sinks with becoming Woe,
Wrapt in a Gown, for Sickness, and for Show.
The Fair-ones feel such Maladies as these,
When each new Night-Dress gives a new Disease.

A constant *Vapour* o'er the Palace flies;
Strange Phantoms rising as the Mists arise;
Dreadful, as Hermit's Dreams in haunted Shades,
Or bright as Visions of expiring Maids.
Now glaring Fiends, and Snakes on rolling Spires,
Pale Spectres, gaping Tombs, and Purple Fires:
Now Lakes of liquid Gold, *Elysian* Scenes,
And Crystal Domes, and Angels in Machines.

Unnumber'd Throngs on ev'ry side are seen
Of Bodies chang'd to various Forms by *Spleen*.
Here living *Teapots* stand, one Arm held out,
One bent; the Handle this, and that the Spout:
A Pipkin there like *Homer*'s *Tripod* walks;
Here sighs a Jar, and there a Goose-pye talks;
Men prove with Child, as pow'rful Fancy works,
And Maids turn'd Bottels, call aloud for Corks.

Safe past the *Gnome* thro' this fantastick Band,
A Branch of healing *Spleenwort* in his hand.
Then thus addrest the Pow'r – Hail wayward Queen!

Who rule the Sex to Fifty from Fifteen,
Parent of Vapours and of Female Wit,
Who give th' *Hysteric* or *Poetic* Fit,
On various Tempers act by various ways,
Make some take Physick, others scribble Plays;
Who cause the Proud their Visits to delay,
And send the Godly in a Pett, to pray.
A Nymph there is, that all thy Pow'r disdains,
And thousands more in equal Mirth maintains.
But oh! if e'er thy *Gnome* could spoil a Grace,
Or raise a Pimple on a beauteous Face,
Like Citron-Waters Matrons' Cheeks inflame,
Or change Complexions at a losing Game;
If e'er with airy Horns I planted Heads,
Or rumpled Petticoats, or tumbled Beds,
Or caus'd Suspicion when no Soul was rude,
Or discompos'd the Head-dress of a Prude,
Or e'er to costive Lap-Dog gave Disease,
Which not the Tears of brightest Eyes could ease:
Hear me, and touch *Belinda* with Chagrin;
That single Act gives half the World the Spleen.

    The Goddess with a discontented Air
Seems to reject him, tho' she grants his Pray'r.
A wondrous Bag with both her Hands she binds,
Like that where once *Ulysses* held the Winds;
There she collects the Force of Female Lungs,
Sighs, Sobs, and Passions, and the War of Tongues.
A Vial next she fills with fainting Fears,
Soft Sorrows, melting Griefs, and flowing Tears.
The *Gnome* rejoicing bears her Gifts away,
Spreads his black Wings, and slowly mounts to Day.

    Sunk in *Thalestris*' Arms the Nymph he found,
Her Eyes dejected and her Hair unbound.
Full o'er their Heads the swelling Bag he rent,
And all the Furies issued at the Vent.
Belinda burns with more than mortal Ire,

And fierce *Thalestris* fans the rising Fire.
O wretched Maid! she spread her Hands, and cry'd,
(While *Hampton*'s Ecchos, wretched Maid! reply'd)
Was it for this you took such constant Care
The *Bodkin, Comb*, and *Essence* to prepare;
For this your Locks in Paper-Durance bound,
For this with tort'ring Irons wreath'd around?
For this with Fillets strain'd your tender Head,
And bravely bore the double Loads of Lead?
Gods! shall the Ravisher display your Hair,
While the Fops envy, and the Ladies stare!
Honour forbid! at whose unrival'd Shrine
Ease, Pleasure, Virtue, All, our Sex resign.
Methinks already I your Tears survey,
Already hear the horrid things they say,
Already see you a degraded Toast,
And all your Honour in a Whisper lost!
How shall I, then, your helpless Fame defend?
'Twill then be Infamy to seem your Friend!
And shall this Prize, th' inestimable Prize,
Expos'd thro' Crystal to the gazing Eyes,
And heighten'd by the Diamond's circling Rays,
On that Rapacious Hand for ever blaze?
Sooner shall Grass in *Hide*-Park *Circus* grow,
And Wits take Lodgings in the Sound of *Bow*;
Sooner let Earth, Air, Sea, to *Chaos* fall,
Men, Monkies, Lap-dogs, Parrots, perish all!
   She said; then raging to *Sir Plume* repairs,
And bids her *Beau* demand the precious Hairs:
(*Sir Plume*, of *Amber Snuff-box* justly vain,
And the nice Conduct of a *clouded Cane*)
With earnest Eyes, and round unthinking Face,
He first the Snuff-box open'd, then the Case,
And thus broke out – 'My Lord, why, what the Devil?
Z – ds! damn the Lock! 'fore Gad, you must be civil!
Plague on't! 'tis past a Jest – nay prithee, Pox!

Give her the Hair' – he spoke, and rapp'd his Box.

   It grieves me much (reply'd the Peer again)
Who speaks so well shou'd ever speak in vain.
But by this Lock, this sacred Lock I swear,
(Which never more shall join its parted Hair,
Which never more its Honours shall renew,
Clipt from the lovely Head where late it grew)
That while my Nostrils draw the vital Air,
This Hand, which won it, shall for ever wear.
He spoke, and speaking, in proud Triumph spread
The long-contended Honours of her Head.

   But *Umbriel*, hateful *Gnome*! forbears not so;
He breaks the Vial whence the Sorrows flow.
Then see! the *Nymph* in beauteous Grief appears,
Her Eyes half-languishing, half-drown'd in Tears;
On her heav'd Bosom hung her drooping Head,
Which, with a Sigh, she rais'd; and thus she said.

   For ever curs'd be this detested Day,
Which snatch'd my best, my fav'rite Curl away!
Happy! ah ten times happy, had I been,
If *Hampton-Court* these Eyes had never seen!
Yet am not I the first mistaken Maid,
By Love of *Courts* to num'rous Ills betray'd.
Oh had I rather un-admir'd remain'd
In some lone Isle, or distant *Northern* Land;
Where the gilt *Chariot* never marks the Way,
Where none learn *Ombre*, none e'er taste *Bohea*!
There kept my Charms conceal'd from mortal Eye,
Like Roses that in Desarts bloom and die.
What mov'd my Mind with youthful Lords to rome?
O had I stay'd, and said my Pray'rs at home!
'Twas this, the Morning *Omens* seem'd to tell;
Thrice from my trembling hand the *Patch-box* fell;
The tott'ring *China* shook without a Wind,
Nay, *Poll* sate mute, and *Shock* was most Unkind!
A *Sylph* too warn'd me of the Threats of Fate,

In mystic Visions, now believ'd too late!
See the poor Remnants of these slighted Hairs!
My hands shall rend what ev'n thy Rapine spares:
These, in two sable Ringlets taught to break,
Once gave new Beauties to the snowie Neck.
The Sister-Lock now sits uncouth, alone,
And in its Fellow's Fate foresees its own;
Uncurl'd it hangs, the fatal Sheers demands;
And tempts once more thy sacrilegious Hands.
Oh hadst thou, Cruel! been content to seize
Hairs less in sight, or any Hairs but these!

CANTO V

She said: the pitying Audience melt in Tears,
But *Fate* and *Jove* had stopp'd the *Baron*'s Ears.
In vain *Thalestris* with Reproach assails,
For who can move when fair *Belinda* fails?
Not half so fixt the *Trojan* cou'd remain,
While *Anna* begg'd and *Dido* rag'd in vain.
Then grave *Clarissa* graceful wav'd her Fan;
Silence ensu'd, and thus the Nymph began.

Say, why are Beauties prais'd and honour'd most,
The wise Man's Passion, and the vain Man's Toast?
Why deck'd with all that Land and Sea afford,
Why Angels call'd, and Angel-like ador'd?
Why round our Coaches crowd the white-glov'd Beaus,
Why bows the Side-box from its inmost Rows?
How vain are all these Glories, all our Pains,
Unless good Sense preserve what Beauty gains:
That Men may say, when we the Front-box grace,
Behold the first in Virtue, as in Face!
Oh! if to dance all Night, and dress all Day,
Charm'd the Small-pox, or chas'd old Age away;
Who would not scorn what Huswife's Cares produce,
Or who would learn one earthly Thing of Use?

To patch, nay ogle, might become a Saint,
Nor could it sure be such a Sin to paint.
But since, alas! frail Beauty must decay,
Curl'd or uncurl'd, since Locks will turn to grey,
Since painted, or not painted, all shall fade,
And she who scorns a Man, must die a Maid;
What then remains, but well our Pow'r to use,
And keep good Humour still whate'er we lose?
And trust me, Dear! good Humour can prevail,
When Airs, and Flights, and Screams, and Scolding fail.
Beauties in vain their pretty Eyes may roll;
Charms strike the Sight, but Merit wins the Soul.

So spoke the Dame, but no Applause ensu'd;
Belinda frown'd, *Thalestris* call'd her Prude.
To Arms, to Arms! the fierce Virago cries,
And swift as Lightning to the Combate flies.
All side in Parties, and begin th' Attack;
Fans clap, Silks russle, and tough Whalebones crack;
Heroes' and Heroins' Shouts confus'dly rise,
And base, and treble Voices strike the Skies.
No common Weapons in their Hands are found,
Like Gods they fight, nor dread a mortal Wound.

So when bold *Homer* makes the Gods engage,
And heav'nly Breasts with human Passions rage;
'Gainst *Pallas, Mars; Latona, Hermes* arms;
And all *Olympus* rings with loud Alarms.
Jove's Thunder roars, Heav'n trembles all around;
Blue *Neptune* storms, the bellowing Deeps resound;
Earth shakes her nodding Tow'rs, the Ground gives way;
And the pale Ghosts start at the Flash of Day!

Triumphant *Umbriel* on a Sconce's Height
Clapt his glad Wings, and sate to view the Fight:
Propt on their Bodkin Spears, the Sprights survey
The growing Combat, or assist the Fray.

While thro' the Press enrag'd *Thalestris* flies,
And scatters Deaths around from both her Eyes,

A *Beau* and *Witling* perish'd in the Throng,
One dy'd in *Metaphor*, and one in *Song*.
O cruel Nymph! a living Death I bear,
Cry'd *Dapperwit*, and sunk beside his Chair.
A mournful Glance Sir *Fopling* upwards cast,
Those Eyes are made so killing – was his last:
Thus on *Meander*'s flow'ry Margin lies
Th' expiring Swan, and as he sings he dies.

    When bold Sir *Plume* had drawn *Clarissa* down,
Chloe stept in, and kill'd him with a Frown;
She smil'd to see the doughty Hero slain,
But at her Smile, the Beau reviv'd again.

    Now *Jove* suspends his golden Scales in Air,
Weighs the Men's Wits against the Lady's Hair;
The doubtful Beam long nods from side to side;
At length the Wits mount up, the Hairs subside.

    See fierce *Belinda* on the *Baron* flies,
With more than usual Lightning in her Eyes;
Nor fear'd the Chief th' unequal Fight to try,
Who sought no more than on his Foe to die.
But this bold Lord, with manly Strength indu'd,
She with one Finger and a Thumb subdu'd:
Just where the Breath of Life his Nostrils drew,
A Charge of *Snuff* the wily Virgin threw;
The *Gnomes* direct, to ev'ry Atome just,
The pungent Grains of titillating Dust.
Sudden, with starting Tears each Eye o'erflows,
And the high Dome re-ecchoes to his Nose.

    Now meet thy Fate, incens'd *Belinda* cry'd,
And drew a deadly *Bodkin* from her Side.
(The same, his ancient Personage to deck,
Her great great Grandsire wore about his Neck
In three *Seal-Rings*; which after, melted down,
Form'd a vast *Buckle* for his Widow's Gown:
Her infant Grandame's *Whistle* next it grew,
The *Bells* she gingled, and the *Whistle* blew;

Then in a *Bodkin* grac'd her Mother's Hairs,
Which long she wore, and now *Belinda* wears.)
   Boast not my Fall (he cry'd) insulting Foe!
Thou by some other shalt be laid as low.
Nor think, to die dejects my lofty Mind;
All that I dread, is leaving you behind!
Rather than so, ah let me still survive,
And burn in *Cupid*'s Flames, – but burn alive.
   Restore the Lock! she cries; and all around
Restore the Lock! the vaulted Roofs rebound.
Not fierce *Othello* in so loud a Strain
Roar'd for the Handkerchief that caus'd his Pain.
But see how oft Ambitious Aims are cross'd,
And Chiefs contend 'till all the Prize is lost!
The Lock, obtain'd with Guilt, and kept with Pain,
In ev'ry place is sought, but sought in vain:
With such a Prize no Mortal must be blest,
So Heav'n decrees! with Heav'n who can contest?
   Some thought it mounted to the Lunar Sphere,
Since all things lost on Earth, are treasur'd there.
There Heroes' Wits are kept in pondrous Vases,
And Beaus' in *Snuff-boxes* and *Tweezer-Cases*.
There broken Vows, and Death-bed Alms are found,
And Lovers' Hearts with Ends of Riband bound;
The Courtier's Promises, and Sick Man's Pray'rs,
The Smiles of Harlots, and the Tears of Heirs,
Cages for Gnats, and Chains to Yoak a Flea;
Dry'd Butterflies, and Tomes of Casuistry.
   But trust the Muse – she saw it upward rise,
Tho' mark'd by none but quick Poetic Eyes:
(So *Rome*'s great Founder to the Heav'ns withdrew,
To *Proculus* alone confess'd in view.)
A sudden Star, it shot thro' liquid Air,
And drew behind a radiant *Trail of Hair*.
Not *Berenice*'s Locks first rose so bright,
The Heav'ns bespangling with dishevel'd Light.

The *Sylphs* behold it kindling as it flies,
And pleas'd pursue its Progress thro' the Skies.
   This the *Beau-monde* shall from the *Mall* survey,
And hail with Musick its propitious Ray.
This, the blest Lover shall for *Venus* take,
And send up Vows from *Rosamonda*'s Lake.
This *Partridge* soon shall view in cloudless Skies,
When next he looks thro' *Galilæo*'s Eyes;
And hence th' Egregious Wizard shall foredoom
The Fate of *Louis*, and the Fall of *Rome*.
   Then cease, bright Nymph! to mourn thy ravish'd Hair
Which adds new Glory to the shining Sphere!
Not all the Tresses that fair Head can boast
Shall draw such Envy as the Lock you lost.
For, after all the Murders of your Eye,
When, after Millions slain, your self shall die;
When those fair Suns shall sett, as sett they must,
And all those Tresses shall be laid in Dust;
This Lock, the Muse shall consecrate to Fame,
And mid'st the Stars inscribe *Belinda*'s Name!

Epistle to Miss Blount, on her leaving the Town, after the Coronation

As some fond virgin, whom her mother's care
Drags from the town to wholsom country air,
Just when she learns to roll a melting eye,
And hear a spark, yet think no danger nigh;
From the dear man unwilling she must sever,
Yet takes one kiss before she parts for ever:
Thus from the world fair *Zephalinda* flew,
Saw others happy, and with sighs withdrew;
Not that their pleasures caus'd her discontent,
She sigh'd not that They stay'd, but that She went.

She went, to plain-work, and to purling brooks,
Old-fashion'd halls, dull aunts, and croaking rooks,
She went from Op'ra, park, assembly, play,
To morning walks, and pray'rs three hours a day;
To pass her time 'twixt reading and Bohea,
To muse, and spill her solitary Tea,
Or o'er cold coffee trifle with the spoon,
Count the slow clock, and dine exact at noon;
Divert her eyes with pictures in the fire,
Hum half a tune, tell stories to the squire;
Up to her godly garret after sev'n,
There starve and pray, for that's the way to heav'n.

Some Squire, perhaps, you take a delight to rack;
Whose game is Whisk, whose treat a toast in sack,
Who visits with a gun, presents you birds,
Then gives a smacking buss, and cries – No words!
Or with his hound comes hollowing from the stable,
Makes love with nods, and knees beneath a table;
Whose laughs are hearty, tho' his jests are coarse,
And loves you best of all things – but his horse.

In some fair evening, on your elbow laid,
You dream of triumphs in the rural shade;

In pensive thought recall the fancy'd scene,
See Coronations rise on ev'ry green;
Before you pass th' imaginary sights
Of Lords, and Earls, and Dukes, and garter'd Knights;
While the spread Fan o'ershades your closing eyes;
Then give one flirt, and all the vision flies.
Thus vanish sceptres, coronets, and balls,
And leave you in lone woods, or empty walls.

　　So when your slave, at some dear, idle time,
(Not plagu'd with headachs, or the want of rhime)
Stands in the streets, abstracted from the crew,
And while he seems to study, thinks of you:
Just when his fancy points your sprightly eyes,
Or sees the blush of soft *Parthenia* rise,
Gay pats my shoulder, and you vanish quite;
Streets, chairs, and coxcombs rush upon my sight;
Vext to be still in town, I knit my brow,
Look sow'r, and hum a tune – as you may now.

A Farewell to London.

Dear, damn'd, distracting Town, farewell!
    Thy Fools no more I'll teize:
This Year in Peace, ye Critics, dwell,
    Ye Harlots, sleep at Ease!

Soft *B*—and rough *C*—*s*, adieu!
    Earl *Warwick* make your Moan,
The lively *H*—*k* and you
    May knock up Whores alone.

To drink and droll be *Rowe* allow'd
    Till the third watchman toll;
Let *Jervase* gratis paint, and *Frowd*
    Save Three-pence, and his Soul.

Farewell *Arbuthnot*'s Raillery
    On every learned Sot;
And *Garth*, the best good Christian he,
    Altho' he knows it not.

Lintot, farewell! thy Bard must go;
    Farewell, unhappy *Tonson*!
Heaven gives thee for thy Loss of *Rowe*,
    Lean *Philips*, and fat *Johnson*.

Why should I stay? Both Parties rage;
    My vixen Mistress squalls;
The Wits in envious Feuds engage;
    And *Homer* (damn him!) calls.

The Love of Arts lies cold and dead
    In *Hallifax*'s Urn;
And not one Muse of all he fed,
    Has yet the Grace to mourn.

My Friends, by Turns, my Friends confound,
    Betray, and are betray'd.
Poor *Y—r*'s sold for Fifty Pound,
    And *B—ll* is a Jade.

Why make I Friendships with the Great,
    When I no Favour seek?
Or follow Girls Seven Hours in Eight?–
    I need but once a Week.

Still idle, with a busy Air,
    Deep Whimsies to contrive;
The gayest Valetudinaire,
    Most thinking Rake alive.

Solicitous for others Ends,
    Tho' fond of dear Repose;
Careless or drowsy with my Friends,
    And frolick with my Foes.

Laborious Lobster-nights, farewell!
    For sober, studious Days;
And *Burlington*'s delicious Meal,
    For Sallads, Tarts, and Pease!

Adieu to all but *Gay* alone,
    Whose Soul, sincere and free,
Loves all Mankind, but flatters none,
    And so may starve with me.

from An Epistle to Henry Cromwell, Esq
   [*lines 49–118*]

   I'm told, you think to take a Step some
Ten Miles from Town, t' a Place call'd *Epsom*,
To treat those Nymphs like yours of *Drury*,
With – I protest, and I'll assure ye;–
But tho' from Flame to Flame you wander,
Beware; your Heart's no *Salamander*!
But burnt so long, may soon turn Tinder,
And so be fir'd by any Cinder-
(Wench, I'd have said did Rhyme not hinder)
Shou'd it so prove, yet who'd admire?
'Tis known, a Cook-maid roasted *Prior*,
Lardella fir'd a famous Author,
And for a Butcher's well-fed Daughter
Great *D—s* roar'd, like Ox at Slaughter.

   (Now, if you're weary of my Style,
Take out your Box of right *Brasil*,
First lay this Paper under, then,
Snuff just three Times, and read again.)

   I had to see you some Intent
But for a curst Impediment,
Which spoils full many a good Design,
That is to say, the Want of Coin.
For which, I had resolv'd almost,
To raise *Tiberius Gracchus* Ghost;
To get, by once more murd'ring *Caius*,
As much as did *Septimuleius*;
But who so dear will buy the Lead,
That lies within a Poet's Head,
As that which in the Hero's Pate
Deserv'd of Gold an equal Weight?

Sir, you're so stiff in your Opinion,
I wish you do not turn *Socinian*;
Or prove Reviver of a Schism,
By modern Wits call'd *Quixotism*.
What mov'd you, pray, without compelling,
Like *Trojan* true, to draw for *Hellen*:
Quarrel with *Dryden* for a Strumpet,
(For so she was, as e'er show'd Rump yet,
Tho' I confess, she had much Grace,
Especially about the Face.)
Virgil, when call'd *Pasiphae Virgo*
(You say) he'd more good Breeding; *Ergo* –
Well argu'd, Faith! Your Point you urge
As home, as ever did *Panurge*:
And one may say of *Dryden* too,
(As once you said of you know who)
He had some Fancy, and cou'd write;
Was very learn'd, but not polite–
However from my Soul I judge
He ne'er (good Man) bore *Hellen* Grudge,
But lov'd her full as well it may be,
As e'er he did his own dear Lady.
You have no Cause to take Offence, Sir,
Z—ds, you're as sour as *Cato Censor*!
Ten times more like him, I profess,
Than I'm like *Aristophanes*.

To end with News – the best I know,
Is, I've been well a Week, or so.
The Season of green Pease is fled,
And Artichoaks reign in their Stead.
Th' Allies to bomb *Toulon* prepare;
G—d save the pretty Lady's there!
One of our Dogs is dead and gone,
And I, unhappy! left alone.

If you have any Consolation
T'administer on this Occasion,
Send it, I pray, by the next Post,
Before my Sorrow be quite lost.
     The twelfth or thirteenth Day of *July*,
     But which, I cannot tell you truly.

Verses Occasion'd by an &c. at the end of
Mr. D'Urfey's Name in the Title to one of his Plays

Jove call's before him t'other Day
The *Vowels, U, O, I, E, A,*
All *Dipthongs*, and all *Consonants*,
Either of *England* or of *France*;
And all that were, or wish'd to be,
Rank'd in the Name of *Tom D'Urfy.*

    Fierce in this Cause, the *Letters* spoke all,
Liquids grew rough, and *Mutes* turn'd vocal:
Those four proud Syllables alone
Were silent, which by Fates Decree
Chim'd in so smoothly, one by one,
To the sweet Name of *Tom D'Urfy.*

    N, by whom Names subsist, declar'd,
To have no Place in this was hard:
And *Q* maintain'd 'twas but his Due
Still to keep Company with *U*;
So hop'd to stand no less than he
In the great Name of *Tom D'Urfy.*

    E shew'd, a *Comma* ne'er could claim
A Place in any *British* Name;
Yet making here a perfect Botch,
Thrusts your poor Vowell from his Notch:
Hiatus mî valde deflendus!
From which good *Jupiter* defend us!
Sooner I'd quit my Part in thee,
Than be no Part in *Tom D'Urfy.*

    P protested, puff'd, and swore,
He'd not be serv'd so like a Beast;
He was a Piece of Emperor,
And made up half a Pope at least.

C vow'd, he'd frankly have releas'd
His double Share in *Cæsar Caius*,
For only one in *Tom Durfeius*.

   I, Consonant and Vowel too,
To *Jupiter* did humbly sue,
That of his Grace he would proclaim
Durfeius his true *Latin* Name;
For tho' without them both, 'twas clear,
Himself could ne'er be *Jupiter*;
Yet they'd resign that Post so high,
To be the Genitive, *Durfei*.

   B and *L* swore Bl— and W—s
X and *Z* cry'd, P—x and Z—s
G swore, by G—d, it ne'er should be;
And *W* would not lose, not he,
An *English Letter*'s Property,
In the great Name of *Tom Durfy*.
Author and he, with equal Grace,
Appear, and stare you in the Face:
Stephens prints *Heathen Greek*, 'tis said,
Which some can't construe, some can't read:
But all that comes from *Lintot*'s Hand
Ev'n *Ra – son* might understand.
Oft in an *Aldus*, or a *Plantin*,
A Page is blotted, or Leaf wanting:
Of *Lintot*'s Books this can't be said,
All fair, and not so much as read.
Their Copy cost 'em not a Penny
To *Homer, Virgil*, or to any;
They ne'er gave *Sixpence* for *two Lines*,
To them, their Heirs, or their Assigns:
But *Lintot* is at vast Expence,
And pays prodigious dear for – Sense.
Their Books are useful but to few,
A Scholar, or a Wit or two:

Lintot's for gen'ral Use are fit;
For some Folks read, but all Folks sh –.

In short, the rest were all in Fray,
From *Christcross* to *Et cætera*.
They, tho' but Standers-by too, mutter'd;
Dipthongs, and Tripthongs, swore and stutter'd,
That none had so much Right to be ⎤
Part of the Name of stuttering *T* – ⎬
T – *Tom* – *a* – *as* – *De* – *Dur* – *fe* – *fy*. ⎦

Then *Jove* thus spake: With Care and Pain
We form'd this Name, renown'd in Rhyme;
Not thine, Immortal *Neufgermain*!
Cost studious *Cabalists* more Time.
Yet now, as then, you all declare, ⎤
Far hence to *Egypt* you'll repair, ⎬
And turn strange Hieroglyphicks there; ⎦
Rather than Letters longer be,
Unless i' th' Name of *Tom D'Urfy*.

Were you all pleas'd, yet what I pray,
To foreign Letters cou'd I say?
What if the *Hebrew* next should aim
To turn quite backward *D'Urfy*'s Name?
Should the *Greek* quarrel too, by *Styx*, I
Cou'd ne'er bring in *Psi* and *Xi*;
Omicron and *Omega* from us
Wou'd each hope to be *O* in *Thomas*;
And all th' ambitious Vowels vie, ⎤
No less than *Pythagorick Y*, ⎬
To have a Place in *Tom D'Urfy*. ⎦

Then, well-belov'd and trusty Letters!
Cons'nants! and Vowels, (much their betters,)
WE, willing to repair this Breach,
And, all that in us lies, please each;
Et cæt'ra to our Aid must call,

Et cæt'ra represents ye all:
Et cæt'ra therefore, we decree,
Henceforth for ever join'd shall be
To the great Name of *Tom Durfy*.

The Court Ballad
To the Tune of 'To all you Ladies now at Land,' &c.

To one fair Lady out of court
   And two fair Ladies in
Who think the Turk and Pope a sport
   And Wit and Love no Sin,
Come these soft lines with nothing Stiff in
To Bellenden Lepell and Griffin
          With a fa.

What passes in the dark third row
   And what behind the Scene,
Couches and crippled Chairs I know,
   And Garrets hung with green;
I know the Swing of sinful Hack,
Where many a Damsel cries oh lack.
          With a fa.

Then why to court should I repair
   Where's such ado with Townsend.
To hear each mortal stamp and swear
   And ev'ry speech in Z—nds end,
To hear 'em rail at honest Sunderland
And rashly blame the realm of Blunderland.
          With a fa.

Alas, like Shutz I cannot pun
   Like Clayton court the Germans
Tell Pickenburg how slim she's grown
   Like Meadows run to sermons,
To court ambitious men may roam,
But I and Marlbro' stay at home.
          With a fa.

In truth by what I can discern,
   Of Courtiers from you Three,

Some Wit you have and more may learn,
    From Court than Gay or me,
Perhaps in time you'll leave High Diet,
And Sup with us on Mirth or Quiet,
                    With a fa.

In Leister fields, in house full nigh,
    With door all painted green,
Where Ribbans wave upon the tye,
    (A Milliner's I ween)
There may you meet us, three to three,
For Gay can well make two of me.
                    With a fa.

But shou'd you catch the Prudish itch,
    And each become a coward,
Bring sometimes with you Lady Rich
    And sometimes Mistress Howard,
For Virgins, to keep chaste, must go
Abroad with such as are not so.
                    With a fa.

And thus fair Maids, my ballad ends,
    God send the King safe landing,
And makes all honest ladies friends,
    To Armies that are Standing.
Preserve the Limits of these nations,
And take off Ladies Limitations.
                    With a fa.

Verses sent to Mrs. T. B. with his Works.

This Book, which, like its Author, You
By the bare Outside only knew,
(Whatever was in either Good,
Not look'd in, or, not understood)
Comes, as the Writer did too long,
To be about you, right or wrong;
Neglected on your Chair to lie,
Nor raise a Thought, nor draw an Eye;
In peevish Fits to have you say,
See there! you're always in my Way!
Or, if your Slave you think to bless,
I like this Colour, I profess!
That Red is charming all will hold,
I ever lov'd it – next to Gold.

   Can Book, or Man, more Praise obtain?
What more could *G—ge* or *S—te* gain?

   Sillier than *Gildon* coud'st thou be,
Nay, did all *Jacob* breath in thee,
She keeps thee, Book! I'll lay my Head,
What? throw away a *Fool in Red*:
No, trust the Sex's sacred Rule;
The gaudy Dress will save the Fool.

Bounce to Fop

An Heroick Epistle from a Dog at Twickenham
to a Dog at Court

To thee, sweet *Fop*, these Lines I send,
Who, tho' no Spaniel, am a Friend.
Tho, once my Tail in wanton play,
Now frisking this, and then that way,
Chanc'd, with a Touch of just the Tip,
To hurt your Lady-lap-dog-ship;
Yet thence to think I'd bite your Head off!
Sure *Bounce* is one you never read of.

Fop! you can dance, and make a Leg,
Can fetch and carry, cringe and beg,
And (what's the Top of all your Tricks)
Can stoop to pick up *Strings* and *Sticks.*
We Country Dogs love nobler Sport,
And scorn the Pranks of Dogs at Court.
Fye, naughty Fop! where e'er you come
To f—t and p—ss about the Room,
To lay your Head in every Lap,
And, when they think not of you – snap!
The worst that Envy, or that Spite
E'er said of me, is, I can bite:
That sturdy Vagrants, Rogues in Rags,
Who poke at me, can make no Brags;
And that to towze such Things as *flutter*,
To honest *Bounce* is Bread and Butter.

While you, and every courtly Fop,
Fawn on the Devil for a Chop,
I've the Humanity to hate
A Butcher, tho' he brings me Meat;
And let me tell you, have a Nose,
(Whatever stinking Fops suppose)

That under Cloth of Gold or Tissue,
Can smell a Plaister, or an Issue.

   Your pilf'ring Lord, with simple Pride,
May wear a Pick-lock at his Side;
My Master wants no Key of State,
For *Bounce* can keep his House and Gate.

   When all such Dogs have had their Days,
As knavish *Pams*, and fawning *Trays*;
When pamper'd *Cupids*, bestly *Veni's*,
And motly, squinting *Harvequini's*,
Shall lick no more their Lady's Br—,
But die of Looseness, Claps, or Itch;
Fair *Thames* from either ecchoing Shoare
Shall hear, and dread my manly Roar.

   See *Bounce*, like *Berecynthia*, crown'd
With thund'ring Offspring all around,
Beneath, beside me, and a top,
A hundred Sons! and not one *Fop*.

   Before my Children set your Beef,
Not one true *Bounce* will be a Thief;
Not one without Permission feed,
(Tho' some of *J*—'s hungry Breed)
But whatsoe'er the Father's Race,
From me they suck a little Grace.
While your fine Whelps learn all to steal,
Bred up by Hand on Chick and Veal.

   My Eldest-born resides not far,
Where shines great *Strafford*'s glittering Star:
My second (Child of Fortune!) waits
At *Burlington*'s Palladian Gates:
A third majestically stalks
(Happiest of Dogs!) in *Cobham*'s Walks;

One ushers Friends to *Bathurst*'s Door;
One fawns, at *Oxford*'s, on the Poor.

Nobles, whom Arms or Arts adorn,
Wait for my Infants yet unborn.
None but a Peer of Wit and Grace,
Can hope a Puppy of my Race.

And O! wou'd Fate the Bliss decree
To mine (a Bliss too great for me)
That two, my tallest Sons, might grace
Attending each with stately Pace,
Iülus' Side, as erst *Evander*'s,
To keep off Flatt'rers, Spies, and Panders,
To let no noble Slave come near,
And scare Lord *Fannys* from his Ear:
Then might a Royal Youth, and true,
Enjoy at least a Friend – or two:
A Treasure, which, of Royal kind,
Few but Himself deserve to find.

Then *Bounce* ('tis all that *Bounce* can crave)
Shall wag her Tail within the Grave.

And tho' no Doctors, Whig, or Tory ones,
Except the Sect of *Pythagoreans*,
Have Immortality assign'd
To any Beast, but *Dryden*'s Hind:
Yet Master *Pope*, whom Truth and Sense
Shall call their Friend some Ages hence,
Tho' now on loftier Themes he sings
Than to bestow a Word on *Kings*,
Has sworn by *Sticks* (the Poet's Oath,
And Dread of Dogs and Poets both)
Man and his Works he'll soon renounce,
And roar in Numbers worthy *Bounce*.

from The Dunciad Variorum.

[*Book I lines 27–76 and 135–212, Book II lines 149–82*]

Where wave the tatter'd ensigns of Rag-Fair,
A yawning ruin hangs and nods in air;
Keen, hollow winds howl thro' the bleak recess,
Emblem of Music caus'd by Emptiness:
Here in one bed two shiv'ring sisters lye,
The cave of Poverty and Poetry.
This, the Great Mother dearer held than all
The clubs of Quidnunc's, or her own Guild-hall.
Here stood her Opium, here she nurs'd her Owls,
And destin'd here th' imperial seat of Fools.
Hence springs each weekly Muse, the living boast
Of Curl's chaste press, and Lintot's rubric post,
Hence hymning Tyburn's elegiac lay,
Hence the soft sing-song on Cecilia's day,
Sepulchral lyes our holy walls to grace,
And New-year Odes, and all the Grubstreet race.
    'Twas here in clouded majesty she shone;
Four guardian Virtues, round, support her Throne;
Fierce champion Fortitude, that knows no fears
Of hisses, blows, or want, or loss of ears:
Calm Temperance, whose blessings those partake
Who hunger, and who thirst, for scribling sake;
Prudence, whose glass presents th' approaching jayl:
Poetic Justice, with her lifted scale;
Where in nice balance, truth with gold she weighs,
And solid pudding against empty praise.
    Here she beholds the Chaos dark and deep,
Where nameless somethings in their causes sleep,
'Till genial Jacob, or a warm Third-day
Call forth each mass, a poem or a play.
How Hints, like spawn, scarce quick in embryo lie,
How new-born Nonsense first is taught to cry,

Maggots half-form'd, in rhyme exactly meet,
And learn to crawl upon poetic feet.
Here one poor Word a hundred clenches makes,
And ductile dulness new meanders takes;
There motley Images her fancy strike,
Figures ill'pair'd, and Similes unlike.
She sees a Mob of Metaphors advance,
Pleas'd with the Madness of the mazy dance:
How Tragedy and Comedy embrace;
How Farce and Epic get a jumbled race;
How Time himself stands still at her command,
Realms shift their place, and Ocean turns to land.
Here gay Description Ægypt glads with showers;
Or gives to Zembla fruits, to Barca flowers;
Glitt'ring with ice here hoary hills are seen,
There painted vallies of eternal green,
On cold December fragrant chaplets blow,
And heavy harvests nod beneath the snow.

                    *

    Of these twelve volumes, twelve of amplest size,
Redeem'd from tapers and defrauded pyes,
Inspir'd he seizes: These an altar raise:
An hecatomb of pure, unsully'd lays
That altar crowns: A folio Common-place
Founds the whole pyle, of all his works the base;
Quarto's, Octavo's shape the less'ning pyre,
And last, a little Ajax tips the spire.
    Then he. 'Great Tamer of all human art!
First in my care, and nearest at my heart:
Dulness! whose good old cause I yet defend,
With whom my Muse began, with whom shall end!
O thou, of business the directing soul,
To human heads like byass to the bowl,
Which as more pond'rous makes their aim more true,
Obliquely wadling to the mark in view.

O ever gracious to perplex'd mankind!
Who spread a healing mist before the mind,
And, lest we err by Wit's wild, dancing light,
Secure us kindly in our native night.
Ah! still o'er Britain stretch that peaceful wand,
Which lulls th' Helvetian and Batavian land.
Where rebel to thy throne if Science rise,
She does but shew her coward face and dies:
There, thy good Scholiasts with unweary'd pains
Make Horace flat, and humble Maro's strains;
Here studious I unlucky moderns save,
Nor sleeps one error in its father's grave,
Old puns restore, lost blunders nicely seek,
And crucify poor Shakespear once a week.
For thee I dim these eyes, and stuff this head,
With all such reading as was never read;
For thee supplying, in the worst of days,
Notes to dull books, and prologues to dull plays;
For thee explain a thing till all men doubt it,
And write about it, Goddess, and about it;
So spins the silkworm small its slender store,
And labours, 'till it clouds itself all o'er.
Not that my quill to Critiques was confin'd,
My Verse gave ampler lessons to mankind;
So gravest precepts may successless prove,
But sad examples never fail to move.
As forc'd from wind-guns, lead itself can fly,
And pond'rous slugs cut swiftly thro' the sky;
As clocks to weight their nimble motion owe,
The wheels above urg'd by the load below;
Me, Emptiness and Dulness could inspire,
And were my Elasticity and Fire.
Had heav'n decreed such works a longer date,
Heav'n had decreed to spare the Grubstreet-state.
But see great Settle to the dust descend,
And all thy cause and empire at an end!

Cou'd Troy be sav'd by any single hand,
His gray-goose-weapon must have made her stand.
But what can I? my Flaccus cast aside,
Take up th' Attorney's (once my better) Guide?
Or rob the Roman geese of all their glories,
And save the state by cackling to the Tories?
Yes, to my Country I my pen consign,
Yes, from this moment, mighty Mist! am thine,
And rival, Curtius! of thy fame and zeal,
O'er head and ears plunge for the publick weal.
Adieu my children! better thus expire
Un-stall'd, unsold; thus glorious mount in fire
Fair without spot; than greas'd by grocer's hands,
Or shipp'd with Ward to ape and monkey lands,
Or wafting ginger, round the streets to go,
And visit alehouse where ye first did grow.'
With that, he lifted thrice the sparkling brand,
And thrice he dropt it from his quiv'ring hand:
Then lights the structure, with averted eyes;
The rowling smokes involve the sacrifice.
The opening clouds disclose each work by turns,
Now flames old Memnon, now Rodrigo burns,
In one quick flash see Proserpine expire,
And last, his own cold Æschylus took fire,
Then gush'd the tears, as from the Trojan's eyes
When the last blaze sent Ilion to the skies.

*

See in the circle next, Eliza plac'd;
Two babes of love close clinging to her waste;
Fair as before her works she stands confess'd,
In flow'rs and pearls by bounteous Kirkall dress'd.
The Goddess then: 'Who best can send on high
The salient spout, far-streaming to the sky;
His be yon Juno of majestic size,
With cow-like-udders, and with ox-like eyes.

This China-Jordan, let the chief o'ercome
Replenish, not ingloriously, at home.'

    Chetwood and Curl accept the glorious strife,
(Tho' one his son dissuades, and one his wife)
This on his manly confidence relies,
That on his vigor and superior size.
First Chetwood lean'd against his letter'd post;
It rose, and labour'd to a curve at most:
So Jove's bright bow displays its watry round,
(Sure sign, that no spectator shall be drown'd).
A second effort brought but new disgrace,
For straining more, it flies in his own face;
Thus the small jett which hasty hands unlock,
Spirts in the gard'ner's eyes who turns the cock.
Not so from shameless Curl: Impetuous spread
The stream, and smoking, flourish'd o'er his head.
So, (fam'd like thee for turbulence and horns,)
Eridanus his humble fountain scorns,
Thro' half the heav'ns he pours th' exalted urn;
His rapid waters in their passage burn.

    Swift as it mounts, all follow with their eyes;
Still happy Impudence obtains the prize.
Thou triumph'st, victor of the high-wrought day,
And the pleas'd dame soft-smiling leads away.
Chetwood, thro' perfect modesty o'ercome,
Crown'd with the Jordan, walks contented home.

Receipt to make Soup. For the Use of Dean Swift

Take a knuckle of Veal
(You may buy it, or steal),
In a few peices cut it,
In a Stewing pan put it,
Salt, pepper and mace
Must season this knuckle,
Then what's join'd to a place,
With other Herbs muckle;
That which killed King Will,
And what never stands still,
Some sprigs of that bed
Where Children are bred,
Which much you will mend, if
Both Spinage and Endive,
And Lettuce and Beet,
With Marygold meet;
Put no water at all;
For it maketh things small;
Which, lest it should happen,
A close cover clap on;
Put this pot of Wood's mettle
In a hot boiling kettle,
And there let it be,
(Mark the Doctrine I teach)
About – let me see, –
Thrice as long as you preach.
So skimming the fat off,
Say Grace, with your hat off
O then, with what rapture
Will it fill Dean and Chapter!

from An Essay on Man

[*Epistle I lines 207–80, Epistle II lines 53–92 and 203–16,
Epistle IV lines 217–58*]

Far as Creation's ample range extends,
The scale of sensual, mental pow'rs ascends:
Mark how it mounts, to Man's imperial race,
From the green myriads in the peopled grass:
What modes of sight betwixt each wide extreme,
The mole's dim curtain, and the lynx's beam:
Of smell, the headlong lioness between,
And hound sagacious on the tainted green:
Of hearing, from the life that fills the flood,
To that which warbles thro' the vernal wood:
The spider's touch, how exquisitely fine!
Feels at each thread, and lives along the line:
In the nice bee, what sense so subtly true
From pois'nous herbs extracts the healing dew:
How Instinct varies in the grov'ling swine,
Compar'd, half-reas'ning elephant, with thine:
'Twixt that, and Reason, what a nice barrier;
For ever sep'rate, yet for ever near!
Remembrance and Reflection how ally'd;
What thin partitions Sense from Thought divide:
And Middle natures, how they long to join,
Yet never pass th' insuperable line!
Without this just gradation, could they be
Subjected these to those, or all to thee?
The pow'rs of all subdu'd by thee alone,
Is not thy Reason all these pow'rs in one?

See, thro' this air, this ocean, and this earth,
All matter quick, and bursting into birth.
Above, how high progressive life may go!
Around, how wide! how deep extend below!
Vast chain of being, which from God began,

Natures æthereal, human, angel, man,
Beast, bird, fish, insect! what no eye can see,
No glass can reach! from Infinite to thee,
From thee to Nothing! – On superior pow'rs
Were we to press, inferior might on ours:
Or in the full creation leave a void,
Where, one step broken, the great scale's destroy'd:
From Nature's chain whatever link you strike,
Tenth or ten thousandth, breaks the chain alike.

    And if each system in gradation roll,
Alike essential to th' amazing whole;
The least confusion but in one, not all
That system only, but the whole must fall.
Let Earth unbalanc'd from her orbit fly,
Planets and Suns run lawless thro' the sky,
Let ruling Angels from their spheres be hurl'd,
Being on being wreck'd, and world on world,
Heav'n's whole foundations to their centre nod,
And Nature tremble to the throne of God:
All this dread ORDER break – for whom? for thee?
Vile worm! – oh Madness, Pride, Impiety!

    What if the foot, ordain'd the dust to tread,
Or hand to toil, aspir'd to be the head?
What if the head, the eye, or ear repin'd
To serve mere engines to the ruling Mind?
Just as absurd for any part to claim
To be another, in this gen'ral frame:
Just as absurd, to mourn the tasks or pains
The great directing MIND of ALL ordains.

    All are but parts of one stupendous whole,
Whose body, Nature is, and God the soul;
That, chang'd thro' all, and yet in all the same,
Great in the earth, as in th' æthereal frame,
Warms in the sun, refreshes in the breeze,
Glows in the stars, and blossoms in the trees,
Lives thro' all life, extends thro' all extent,

Spreads undivided, operates unspent,
Breathes in our soul, informs our mortal part,
As full, as perfect, in a hair as heart;
As full, as perfect, in vile Man that mourns,
As the rapt Seraph that adores and burns;
To him no high, no low, no great, no small;
He fills, he bounds, connects, and equals all.

*

Two Principles in human nature reign;
Self-love, to urge, and Reason, to restrain;
Nor this a good, nor that a bad we call,
Each works its end, to move or govern all:
And to their proper operation still,
Ascribe all Good; to their improper, Ill.
Self-love, the spring of motion, acts the soul;
Reason's comparing balance rules the whole.
Man, but for that, no action could attend,
And, but for this, were active to no end;
Fix'd like a plant on his peculiar spot,
To draw nutrition, propagate, and rot;
Or, meteor-like, flame lawless thro' the void,
Destroying others, by himself destroy'd.
Most strength the moving principle requires;
Active its task, it prompts, impels, inspires.
Sedate and quiet the comparing lies,
Form'd but to check, delib'rate, and advise.
Self-love still stronger, as its objects nigh;
Reason's at distance, and in prospect lie:
That sees immediate good by present sense;
Reason, the future and the consequence.
Thicker than arguments, temptations throng,
At best more watchful this, but that more strong.
The action of the stronger to suspend
Reason still use, to Reason still attend:
Attention, habit and experience gains,
Each strengthens Reason, and Self-love restrains.

Let subtle schoolmen teach these friends to fight,
More studious to divide than to unite,
And Grace and Virtue, Sense and Reason split,
With all the rash dexterity of Wit:
Wits, just like fools, at war about a Name,
Have full as oft no meaning, or the same.
Self-love and Reason to one end aspire,
Pain their aversion, Pleasure their desire;
But greedy that its object would devour,
This taste the honey, and not wound the flow'r:
Pleasure, or wrong or rightly understood,
Our greatest evil, or our greatest good.

*

This light and darkness in our chaos join'd,
What shall divide? The God within the mind.
Extremes in Nature equal ends produce,
In Man they join to some mysterious use;
Tho' each by turns the other's bound invade,
As, in some well-wrought picture, light and shade,
And oft so mix, the diff'rence is too nice
Where ends the Virtue, or begins the Vice.
Fools! who from hence into the notion fall,
That Vice or Virtue there is none at all.
If white and black blend, soften, and unite
A thousand ways, is there no black or white?
Ask your own heart, and nothing is so plain;
'Tis to mistake them, costs the time and pain.

*

Look next on Greatness; say where Greatness lies?
'Where, but among the Heroes and the Wise?'
Heroes are much the same, the point's agreed,
From Macedonia's madman to the Swede;
The whole strange purpose of their lives, to find
Or make, an enemy of all mankind!
Not one looks backward, onward still he goes,

Yet ne'er looks forward farther than his nose.
No less alike the Politic and Wise,
All sly slow things, with circumspective eyes:
Men in their loose unguarded hours they take,
Not that themselves are wise, but others weak.
But grant that those can conquer, these can cheat,
'Tis phrase absurd to call a Villain Great:
Who wickedly is wise, or madly brave,
Is but the more a fool, the more a knave.
Who noble ends by noble means obtains,
Or failing, smiles in exile or in chains,
Like good Aurelius let him reign, or bleed
Like Socrates, that Man is great indeed.
What's Fame? a fancy'd life in others breath,
A thing beyond us, ev'n before our death.
Just what you hear, you have, and what's unknown
The same (my Lord) if Tully's or your own.
All that we feel of it begins and ends
In the small circle of our foes or friends;
To all beside as much an empty shade,
An Eugene living, as a Cæsar dead,
Alike or when, or where, they shone, or shine,
Or on the Rubicon, or on the Rhine.
A Wit's a feather, and a Chief a rod;
An honest Man's the noblest work of God.
Fame but from death a villain's name can save,
As Justice tears his body from the grave,
When what t'oblivion better were resign'd,
Is hung on high, to poison half mankind.
All fame is foreign, but of true desert,
Plays round the head, but comes not to the heart:
One self-approving hour whole years out-weighs
Of stupid starers, and of loud huzzas;
And more true joy Marcellus exil'd feels,
Than Cæsar with a senate at his heels.

from Moral Essays: Epistle to Allen Lord Bathurst

Who shall decide, when Doctors disagree,
And soundest Casuists doubt, like you and me?
You hold the word, from Jove to Momus giv'n,
That Man was made the standing jest of Heav'n;
And Gold but sent to keep the fools in play,
For some to heap, and some to throw away.

  But I, who think more highly of our kind,
(And surely, Heav'n and I are of a mind)
Opine, that Nature, as in duty bound,
Deep hid the shining mischief under ground:
But when by Man's audacious labour won,
Flam'd forth this rival to, its Sire, the Sun,
Then careful Heav'n supply'd two sorts of Men,
To squander these, and those to hide agen.

  Like Doctors thus, when much dispute has past,
We find our tenets just the same at last.
Both fairly owning, Riches in effect
No grace of Heav'n or token of th' Elect;
Giv'n to the Fool, the Mad, the Vain, the Evil,
To Ward, to Waters, Chartres, and the Devil.

  What Nature wants, commodious Gold bestows,
'Tis thus we eat the bread another sows:
But how unequal it bestows, observe,
'Tis thus we riot, while who sow it, starve.
What Nature wants (a phrase I much distrust)
Extends to Luxury, extends to Lust:
And if we count among the Needs of life
Another's Toil, why not another's Wife?
Useful, I grant, it serves what life requires,
But dreadful too, the dark Assassin hires:
Trade it may help, Society extend;
But lures the Pyrate, and corrupts the Friend:
It raises Armies in a Nation's aid,

But bribes a Senate, and the Land's betray'd.
Oh! that such bulky Bribes as all might see,
Still, as of old, incumber'd Villainy!
In vain may Heroes fight, and Patriots rave;
If secret Gold saps on from knave to knave.
Could France or Rome divert our brave designs,
With all their brandies or with all their wines?
What could they more than Knights and Squires confound,
Or water all the Quorum ten miles round?
A Statesman's slumbers how this speech would spoil!
'Sir, Spain has sent a thousand jars of oil;
Huge bales of British cloth blockade the door;
A hundred oxen at your levee roar.'

   Poor Avarice one torment more would find;
Nor could Profusion squander all in kind.
Astride his cheese Sir Morgan might we meet,
And Worldly crying coals from street to street,
(Whom with a wig so wild, and mien so maz'd,
Pity mistakes for some poor tradesman craz'd).
Had Colepepper's whole wealth been hops and hogs,
Could he himself have sent it to the dogs?
His Grace will game: to White's a Bull be led,
With spurning heels and with a butting head.
To White's be carried, as to ancient games,
Fair Coursers, Vases, and alluring Dames.
Shall then Uxorio, if the stakes he sweep,
Bear home six Whores, and make his Lady weep?
Or soft Adonis, so perfum'd and fine,
Drive to St. James's a whole herd of swine?
Oh filthy check on all industrious skill,
To spoil the nation's last great trade, Quadrille!

   Once, we confess, beneath the Patriot's cloak,
From the crack'd bag the dropping Guinea spoke,
And gingling down the back-stairs, told the crew,
'Old Cato is as great a Rogue as you.'
Blest paper-credit! last and best supply!

That lends Corruption lighter wings to fly!
Gold imp'd by thee, can compass hardest things,
Can pocket States, can fetch or carry Kings;
A single leaf shall waft an Army o'er,
Or ship off Senates to a distant Shore;
A leaf, like Sibyl's, scatter to and fro
Our fates and fortunes, as the winds shall blow:
Pregnant with thousands flits the Scrap unseen,
And silent sells a King, or buys a Queen.
   Since then, my Lord, on such a World we fall,
What say you? 'Say? Why take it, Gold and all.'
   What Riches give us let us then enquire:
Meat, Fire, and Cloaths. What more? Meat, Cloaths, and Fire.
Is this too little? would you more than live?
Alas! 'tis more than Turner finds they give.
Alas! 'tis more than (all his Visions past)
Unhappy Wharton, waking, found at last!
What can they give? to dying Hopkins Heirs;
To Chartres, Vigour; Japhet, Nose and Ears?
Can they, in gems bid pallid Hippia glow,
In Fulvia's buckle ease the throbs below,
Or heal, old Narses, thy obscener ail,
With all th' embroid'ry plaister'd at thy tail?
They might (were Harpax not too wise to spend)
Give Harpax self the blessing of a Friend;
Or find some Doctor that would save the life
Of wretched Shylock, spite of Shylock's Wife:
But thousands die, without or this or that,
Die, and endow a College, or a Cat:
To some, indeed, Heav'n grants the happier fate,
T' enrich a Bastard, or a Son they hate.
   Perhaps you think the Poor might have their part?
Bond damns the Poor, and hates them from his heart:
The grave Sir Gilbert holds it for a rule,
That 'every man in want is knave or fool:'
'God cannot love (says Blunt, with tearless eyes)

The wretch he starves' – and piously denies:
But the good Bishop, with a meeker air,
Admits, and leaves them Providence's care.

   Yet, to be just to these poor men of pelf,
Each does but hate his Neighbour as himself:
Damn'd to the Mines, an equal fate betides
The Slave that digs it, and the Slave that hides.
Who suffer thus, mere Charity should own,
Must act on motives pow'rful, tho' unknown:
Some War, some Plague, or Famine they foresee,
Some Revelation hid from you and me.
Why Shylock wants a meal, the cause is found,
He thinks a Loaf will rise to fifty pound.
What made Directors cheat in South-sea year?
To live on Ven'son when it sold so dear.
Ask you why Phryne the whole Auction buys?
Phryne foresees a general Excise.
Why she and Sappho raise that monstrous sum?
Alas! they fear a man will cost a plum.

   Wise Peter sees the World's respect for Gold,
And therefore hopes this Nation may be sold:
Glorious Ambition! Peter, swell thy store,
And be what Rome's great Didius was before.

   The Crown of Poland, venal twice an age,
To just three millions stinted modest Gage.
But nobler scenes Maria's dreams unfold,
Hereditary Realms, and worlds of Gold.
Congenial souls! whose life one Av'rice joins,
And one fate buries in th' Asturian Mines.

   Much injur'd Blunt! why bears he Britain's hate?
A wizard told him in these words our fate:
'At length Corruption, like a gen'ral flood,
(So long by watchful Ministers withstood)
Shall deluge all; and Av'rice creeping on,
Spread like a low-born mist, and blot the Sun;
Statesman and Patriot ply alike the stocks,

Peeress and Butler share alike the Box,
And Judges job, and Bishops bite the town,
And mighty Dukes pack cards for half a crown.
See Britain sunk in lucre's sordid charms,
And France reveng'd of ANNE's and EDWARD's arms!'
No mean Court-badge, great Scriv'ner! fir'd thy
   brain,
Nor lordly Luxury, nor City Gain:
No, 'twas thy righteous end, asham'd to see
Senates degen'rate, Patriots disagree,
And nobly wishing Party-rage to cease,
To buy both sides, and give thy Country peace.

  'All this is madness,' cries a sober sage:
But who, my friend, has reason in his rage?

  'The ruling Passion, be it what it will,
The ruling Passion conquers Reason still.'
Less mad the wildest whimsey we can frame,
Than ev'n that Passion, if it has no Aim;
For tho' such motives Folly you may call,
The Folly's greater to have none at all.

  Hear then the truth: ' 'Tis Heav'n each Passion sends,
And diff'rent men directs to diff'rent ends.
Extremes in Nature equal good produce,
Extremes in Man concur to gen'ral use.'
Ask we what makes one keep, and one bestow?
That POW'R who bids the Ocean ebb and flow,
Bids seed-time, harvest, equal course maintain,
Thro' reconcil'd extremes of drought and rain,
Builds Life on Death, on Change Duration founds,
And gives th' eternal wheels to know their rounds.

  Riches, like insects, when conceal'd they lie,
Wait but for wings, and in their season, fly.
Who sees pale Mammon pine amidst his store,
Sees but a backward steward for the Poor;
This year a Reservoir, to keep and spare,
The next a Fountain, spouting thro' his Heir,

In lavish streams to quench a Country's thirst,
And men and dogs shall drink him 'till they burst.

  Old Cotta sham'd his fortune and his birth,
Yet was not Cotta void of wit or worth:
What tho' (the use of barb'rous spits forgot)
His kitchen vy'd in coolness with his grot?
His court with nettles, moats with cresses stor'd,
With soups unbought and sallads blest his board.
If Cotta liv'd on pulse, it was no more
Than Bramins, Saints, and Sages did before;
To cram the Rich was prodigal expence,
And who would take the Poor from Providence?
Like some lone Chartreux stands the good old Hall,
Silence without, and Fasts within the wall;
No rafter'd roofs with dance and tabor sound,
No noontide-bell invites the country round;
Tenants with sighs the smoakless tow'rs survey,
And turn th' unwilling steeds another way:
Benighted wanderers, the forest o'er,
Curse the sav'd candle, and unop'ning door;
While the gaunt mastiff growling at the gate,
Affrights the beggar whom he longs to eat.

  Not so his Son, he mark'd this oversight,
And then mistook reverse of wrong for right.
(For what to shun will no great knowledge need,
But what to follow, is a task indeed.)
What slaughter'd hecatombs, what floods of wine,
Fill the capacious Squire, and deep Divine!
Yet no mean motive this profusion draws,
His oxen perish in his country's cause;
'Tis GEORGE and LIBERTY that crowns the cup,
And Zeal for that great House which eats him up.
The woods recede around the naked seat,
The Sylvans groan – no matter – for the Fleet:
Next goes his Wool – to clothe our valiant bands,
Last, for his Country's love, he sells his Lands.

To town he comes, completes the nation's hope,
And heads the bold Train-bands, and burns a Pope.
And shall not Britain now reward his toils,
Britain, that pays her Patriots with her Spoils?
In vain at Court the Bankrupt pleads his cause,
His thankless Country leaves him to her Laws.

    The Sense to value Riches, with the Art
T'enjoy them, and the Virtue to impart,
Not meanly, nor ambitiously pursu'd,
Not sunk by sloth, nor rais'd by servitude;
To balance Fortune by a just expence,
Join with Oeconomy, Magnificence;
With Splendour, Charity; with Plenty, Health;
Oh teach us, BATHURST! yet unspoil'd by wealth!
That secret rare, between th' extremes to move
Of mad Good-nature, and of mean Self-love.

    To Want or Worth well-weigh'd, be Bounty giv'n,
And ease, or emulate, the care of Heav'n,
Whose measure full o'erflows on human race;
Mend Fortune's fault, and justify her grace.
Wealth in the gross is death, but life diffus'd,
As Poison heals, in just proportion us'd:
In heaps, like Ambergrise, a stink it lies,
But well-dispers'd, is Incense to the Skies.

    Who starves by Nobles, or with Nobles eats?
The Wretch that trusts them, and the Rogue that cheats.
Is there a Lord, who knows a cheerful noon
Without a Fiddler, Flatt'rer, or Buffoon?
Whose table, Wit, or modest Merit share,
Un-elbow'd by a Gamester, Pimp, or Play'r?
Who copies Your's, or OXFORD's better part,
To ease th' oppress'd, and raise the sinking heart?
Where-e'er he shines, oh Fortune, gild the scene,
And Angels guard him in the golden Mean!
There, English Bounty yet a-while may stand,
And Honour linger ere it leaves the land.

But all our praises why should Lords engross?
Rise, honest Muse! and sing the MAN of ROSS:
Pleas'd Vaga echoes thro' her winding bounds,
And rapid Severn hoarse applause resounds.
Who hung with woods yon mountain's sultry brow?
From the dry rock who bade the waters flow?
Not to the skies in useless columns tost,
Or in proud falls magnificently lost,
But clear and artless, pouring thro' the plain
Health to the sick, and solace to the swain.
Whose Cause-way parts the vale with shady rows?
Whose Seats the weary Traveller repose?
Who taught that heav'n-directed spire to rise?
The MAN of ROSS, each lisping babe replies.
Behold the Market-place with poor o'erspread!
The MAN of ROSS divides the weekly bread:
Behold yon Alms-house, neat, but void of state,
Where Age and Want sit smiling at the gate:
Him portion'd maids, apprentic'd orphans blest,
The young who labour, and the old who rest.
Is any sick? the MAN of ROSS relieves,
Prescribes, attends, the med'cine makes, and gives.
Is there a variance? enter but his door,
Balk'd are the Courts, and contest is no more.
Despairing Quacks with curses fled the place,
And vile Attornies, now an useless race.

   'Thrice happy man! enabled to pursue
What all so wish, but want the pow'r to do!
Oh say, what sums that gen'rous hand supply?
What mines, to swell that boundless charity?'

   Of Debts, and Taxes, Wife and Children clear,
This man possest – five hundred pounds a year.
Blush, Grandeur, blush! proud Courts, withdraw your blaze!
Ye little Stars! hide your diminish'd rays.

   'And what? no monument, inscription, stone?
His race, his form, his name almost unknown?'

Who builds a Church to God, and not to Fame,
Will never mark the marble with his Name:
Go, search it there, where to be born and die,
Of rich and poor makes all the history;
Enough, that Virtue fill'd the space between;
Prov'd, by the ends of being, to have been.
When Hopkins dies, a thousand lights attend
The wretch, who living sav'd a candle's end:
Should'ring God's altar a vile image stands,
Belies his features, nay extends his hands;
That live-long wig which Gorgon's self might own,
Eternal buckle takes in Parian stone.
Behold what blessing Wealth to life can lend!
And see, what comfort it affords our end.

   In the worst inn's worst room, with mat half-hung,
The floors of plaister, and the walls of dung,
On once a flock-bed, but repair'd with straw,
With tape-ty'd curtains, never meant to draw,
The George and Garter dangling from that bed
Where tawdry yellow strove with dirty red,
Great Villiers lies – alas! how chang'd from him,
That life of pleasure, and that soul of whim!
Gallant and gay, in Cliveden's proud alcove,
The bow'r of wanton Shrewsbury and love;
Or just as gay, at Council, in a ring
Of mimick'd Statesmen, and their merry King.
No Wit to flatter, left of all his store!
No Fool to laugh at, which he valu'd more.
There, Victor of his health, of fortune, friends,
And fame; this lord of useless thousands ends.

   His Grace's fate sage Cutler could foresee,
And well (he thought) advis'd him, 'Live like me.'
As well his Grace reply'd, 'Like you, Sir John?
That I can do, when all I have is gone.'
Resolve me, Reason, which of these is worse,
Want with a full, or with an empty purse?

Thy life more wretched, Cutler, was confess'd,
Arise, and tell me, was thy death more bless'd?
Cutler saw tenants break, and houses fall,
For very want; he could not build a wall.
His only daughter in a stranger's pow'r,
For very want; he could not pay a dow'r.
A few grey hairs his rev'rend temples crown'd,
'Twas very want that sold them for two pound.
What ev'n deny'd a cordial at his end,
Banish'd the doctor, and expell'd the friend?
What but a want, which you perhaps think mad,
Yet numbers feel, the want of what he had.
Cutler and Brutus, dying both exclaim,
'Virtue! and Wealth! what are ye but a name!'

Say, for such worth are other worlds prepar'd?
Or are they both, in this their own reward?
A knotty point! to which we now proceed.
But you are tir'd – I'll tell a tale. 'Agreed.'

Where London's column, pointing at the skies,
Like a tall bully, lifts the head, and lyes;
There dwelt a Citizen of sober fame,
A plain good man, and Balaam was his name;
Religious, punctual, frugal, and so forth;
His word would pass for more than he was worth.
One solid dish his week-day meal affords,
An added pudding solemniz'd the Lord's:
Constant at Church, and Change; his gains were sure,
His givings rare, save farthings to the poor.

The Dev'l was piqu'd such saintship to behold,
And long'd to tempt him like good Job of old:
But Satan now is wiser than of yore,
And tempts by making rich, not making poor.

Rouz'd by the Prince of Air, the whirlwinds sweep
The surge, and plunge his Father in the deep;
Then full against his Cornish lands they roar,
And two rich ship-wrecks bless the lucky shore.

Sir Balaam now, he lives like other folks,
He takes his chirping pint, and cracks his jokes:
'Live like yourself,' was soon my Lady's word;
And lo! two puddings smoak'd upon the board.

Asleep and naked as an Indian lay,
An honest factor stole a Gem away:
He pledg'd it to the knight; the knight had wit,
So kept the Diamond, and the rogue was bit.
Some scruple rose, but thus he eas'd his thought,
'I'll now give six-pence where I gave a groat,
Where once I went to church, I'll now go twice –
And am so clear too of all other vice.'

The Tempter saw his time; the work he ply'd;
Stocks and Subscriptions pour on ev'ry side,
'Till all the Dæmon makes his full descent,
In one abundant show'r of Cent. per Cent.,
Sinks deep within him, and possesses whole,
Then dubs Director, and secures his soul.

Behold Sir Balaam, now a man of spirit,
Ascribes his gettings to his parts and merit,
What late he call'd a Blessing, now was Wit,
And God's good Providence, a lucky Hit.
Things change their titles, as our manners turn:
His Compting-house employ'd the Sunday-morn;
Seldom at Church ('twas such a busy life)
But duly sent his family and wife.
There (so the Dev'l ordain'd) one Christmas-tide
My good old Lady catch'd a cold, and dy'd.

A Nymph of Quality admires our Knight;
He marries, bows at Court, and grows polite:
Leaves the dull Cits, and joins (to please the fair)
The well-bred cuckolds in St. James's air:
First, for his Son a gay Commission buys,
Who drinks, whores, fights, and in a duel dies:
His daughter flaunts a Viscount's tawdry wife;
She bears a Coronet and P–x for life.

In Britain's Senate he a seat obtains,
And one more Pensioner St. Stephen gains.
My Lady falls to play; so bad her chance,
He must repair it; takes a bribe from France;
The House impeach him; Coningsby harangues;
The Court forsake him, and Sir Balaam hangs:
Wife, son, and daughter, Satan, are thy own,
His wealth, yet dearer, forfeit to the Crown:
The Devil and the King divide the prize,
And sad Sir Balaam curses God and dies.

from Moral Essays: Epistle to Richard Boyle,
Earl of Burlington
[*lines 99–176*]

At Timon's Villa let us pass a day,
Where all cry out, 'What sums are thrown away!'
So proud, so grand, of that stupendous air,
Soft and Agreeable come never there.
Greatness, with Timon, dwells in such a draught
As brings all Brobdignag before your thought.
To compass this, his building is a Town,
His pond an Ocean, his parterre a Down:
Who but must laugh, the Master when he sees,
A puny insect, shiv'ring at a breeze!
Lo, what huge heaps of littleness around!
The whole, a labour'd Quarry above ground.
Two Cupids squirt before: a Lake behind
Improves the keenness of the Northern wind.
His Gardens next your admiration call,
On ev'ry side you look, behold the Wall!
No pleasing Intricacies intervene,
No artful wildness to perplex the scene;
Grove nods at grove, each Alley has a brother,
And half the platform just reflects the other.
The suff'ring eye inverted Nature sees,
Trees cut to Statues, Statues thick as trees,
With here a Fountain, never to be play'd,
And there a Summer-house, that knows no shade;
Here Amphitrite sails thro' myrtle bow'rs;
There Gladiators fight, or die, in flow'rs;
Un-water'd see the drooping sea-horse mourn,
And swallows roost in Nilus' dusty Urn.
My Lord advances with majestic mien,
Smit with the mighty pleasure, to be seen:
But soft – by regular approach – not yet–

First thro' the length of yon hot Terrace sweat,
And when up ten steep slopes you've dragg'd your thighs,
Just at his Study-door he'll bless your eyes.

His Study! with what Authors is it stor'd?
In Books, not Authors, curious is my Lord;
To all their dated Backs he turns you round,
These Aldus printed, those Du Suëil has bound.
Lo some are Vellom, and the rest as good
For all his Lordship knows, but they are Wood.
For Locke or Milton 'tis in vain to look,
These shelves admit not any modern book.

And now the Chapel's silver bell you hear,
That summons you to all the Pride of Pray'r:
Light quirks of Musick, broken and uneven,
Make the soul dance upon a Jig to Heaven.
On painted Cielings you devoutly stare,
Where sprawl the Saints of Verrio or Laguerre,
On gilded clouds in fair expansion lie,
And bring all Paradise before your eye.
To rest, the Cushion and soft Dean invite,
Who never mentions Hell to ears polite.

But hark! the chiming Clocks to dinner call;
A hundred footsteps scrape the marble Hall:
The rich Buffet well-colour'd Serpents grace,
And gaping Tritons spew to wash your face.
Is this a dinner? this a Genial room?
No, 'tis a Temple, and a Hecatomb.
A solemn Sacrifice, perform'd in state,
You drink by measure, and to minutes eat.
So quick retires each flying course, you'd swear
Sancho's dread Doctor and his Wand were there.
Between each Act the trembling salvers ring,
From soup to sweet-wine, and God bless the King.
In plenty starving, tantaliz'd in state,
And complaisantly help'd to all I hate,
Treated, caress'd, and tir'd, I take my leave,

Sick of his civil Pride from Morn to Eve;
I curse such lavish cost, and little skill,
And swear no Day was ever past so ill.

Yet hence the Poor are cloath'd, the Hungry fed;
Health to himself, and to his Infants bread
The Lab'rer bears: What his hard Heart denies,
His charitable Vanity supplies.

Another age shall see the golden Ear
Imbrown the Slope, and nod on the Parterre,
Deep Harvests bury all his pride has plann'd,
And laughing Ceres re-assume the land.

from An Epistle from Mr Pope, to Dr Arbuthnot
[*lines 305–34*]

Let *Sporus* tremble – 'What? that Thing of silk,
Sporus, that mere white Curd of Ass's milk?
Satire or Sense alas! can *Sporus* feel?
Who breaks a Butterfly upon a Wheel?'
Yet let me flap this Bug with gilded wings,
This painted Child of Dirt that stinks and stings;
Whose Buzz the Witty and the Fair annoys,
Yet Wit ne'er tastes, and Beauty ne'er enjoys,
So well-bred Spaniels civilly delight
In mumbling of the Game they dare not bite.
Eternal Smiles his Emptiness betray,
As shallow streams run dimpling all the way.
Whether in florid Impotence he speaks,
And, as the Prompter breathes, the Puppet squeaks;
Or at the Ear of *Eve*, familiar Toad,
Half Froth, half Venom, spits himself abroad,
In Puns, or Politicks, or Tales, or Lyes,
Or Spite, or Smut, or Rymes, or Blasphemies.
His Wit all see-saw between *that* and *this*,
Now high, now low, now Master up, now Miss,
And he himself one vile Antithesis.
Amphibious Thing! that acting either Part,
The trifling Head, or the corrupted Heart!
Fop at the Toilet, Flatt'rer at the Board,
Now trips a Lady, and now struts a Lord.
Eve's Tempter thus the Rabbins have exprest,
A Cherub's face, a Reptile all the rest;
Beauty that shocks you, Parts that none will trust,
Wit that can creep, and Pride that licks the dust.

The Second Satire of the Second Book of
Horace Paraphrased

What, and how great, the Virtue and the Art
To live on little with a chearful heart,
(A Doctrine sage, but truly none of mine)
Lets talk, my friends, but talk before we dine:
Not when a gilt Buffet's reflected pride
Turns you from sound Philosophy aside;
Not when from Plate to Plate your eyeballs roll,
And the brain dances to the mantling bowl.

    Hear Bethel's Sermon, one not vers'd in schools,
But strong in sense, and wise without the rules.

    Go work, hunt, exercise! (he thus began)
Then scorn a homely dinner, if you can.
Your wine lock'd up, your Butler stroll'd abroad,
Or fish deny'd, (the River yet un-thaw'd)
If then plain Bread and milk will do the feat,
The pleasure lies in *you*, and not the meat.
Preach as I please, I doubt our curious men
Will chuse a *Pheasant* still before a *Hen*;
Yet Hens of *Guinea* full as good I hold,
Except you eat the feathers, green and gold.
Of *Carps* and *Mullets* why prefer the *great*,
(Tho' cut in pieces e'er my Lord can eat)
Yet for *small Turbots* such esteem profess?
Because God made these large, the other less.

    Oldfield, with more than Harpy throat endu'd,
Cries, 'Send me, Gods! a whole Hog *barbecu'd!*'
Oh blast it, South-winds! till a stench exhale,
Rank as the ripeness of a Rabbit's tail.
By what *Criterion* do ye eat, d'ye think,
If this is priz'd for *sweetness*, that for *stink*?
When the tir'd Glutton labours thro' a Treat,
He finds no relish in the sweetest Meat;

He calls for something bitter, something sour,
And the rich feast concludes extremely poor:
Cheap eggs, and herbs, and olives still we see,
Thus much is left of old Simplicity!

The *Robin-red-breast* till of late had rest,
And children sacred held a *Martin*'s nest,
Till *Becca-ficos* sold so dev'lish dear
To one that was, or would have been a Peer.
Let me extoll a *Cat* on Oysters fed,
I'll have a Party at the *Bedford Head*,
Or ev'n to crack live *Crawfish* recommend,
I'd never doubt at Court to make a Friend.

'Tis yet in vain, I own, to keep a pother
About one Vice, and fall into the other:
Between Excess and Famine lies a mean,
Plain, but not sordid, tho' not splendid, clean.
Avidien or his Wife (no matter which,
For him you'll call a dog, and her a bitch)
Sell their presented Partridges, and Fruits,
And humbly live on rabbits and on roots:
One half-pint bottle serves them both to dine,
And is at once their vinegar and wine.
But on some lucky day (as when they found
A lost Bank-bill, or heard their Son was drown'd)
At such a feast old vinegar to spare,
Is what two souls so gen'rous cannot bear;
Oyl, tho' it stink, they drop by drop impart,
But sowse the Cabbidge with a bounteous heart.

He knows to live, who keeps the middle state,
And neither leans on this side, nor on that:
Nor stops, for one bad Cork, his Butler's pay,
Swears, like Albutius, a good Cook away;
Nor lets, like Nævius, ev'ry error pass,
The musty wine, foul cloth, or greasy glass.

Now hear what blessings Temperance can bring:
(Thus said our Friend, and what he said I sing.)

First Health: The stomach (cram'd from ev'ry dish,
A Tomb of boil'd, and roast, and flesh, and fish,
Where Bile, and wind, and phlegm, and acid jar,
And all the Man is one intestine war)
Remembers oft the School-boy's simple fare,
The temp'rate sleeps, and spirits light as air!
   How pale, each Worshipful and rev'rend Guest
Rise from a Clergy, or a City, feast!
What life in all that ample Body say,
What heav'nly Particle inspires the clay?
The Soul subsides; and wickedly inclines
To seem but mortal, ev'n in sound Divines.
On morning wings how active springs the Mind,
That leaves the load of yesterday behind?
How easy ev'ry labour it pursues?
How coming to the Poet ev'ry Muse?
Not but we may exceed, some Holy time,
Or tir'd in search of Truth, or search of Rhyme.
Ill Health some just indulgence may engage,
And more, the Sickness of long Life, Old-age:
For fainting Age what cordial drop remains,
If our intemp'rate Youth the Vessel drains?

   Our Fathers prais'd rank Ven'son. You suppose
Perhaps, young men! our Fathers had no nose?
Not so: a Buck was then a week's repast,
And 'twas their point, I ween, to make it last:
More pleas'd to keep it till their friends could come,
Than eat the sweetest by themselves at home.
Why had not I in those good times my birth,
E're Coxcomb-pyes or Coxcombs were on earth?
   Unworthy He, the voice of Fame to hear,
(That sweetest Music to an honest ear;
For 'faith Lord Fanny! you are in the wrong,
The World's good word is better than a Song)
Who has not learn'd, fresh Sturgeon and Ham-pye

Are no rewards for Want, and Infamy!
When Luxury has lick'd up all thy pelf,
Curs'd by thy neighbours, thy Trustees, thy self,
To friends, to fortune, to mankind a shame,
Think how Posterity will treat thy name;
And buy a Rope, that future times may tell
Thou hast at least bestow'd one penny well.

   'Right, cries his Lordship, for a Rogue in need
To have a Taste, is Insolence indeed:
In me 'tis noble, suits my birth and state,
My wealth unwieldy, and my heap too great.'
Then, like the Sun, let Bounty spread her ray,
And shine that Superfluity away.
Oh Impudence of wealth! with all thy store,
How dar'st thou let one worthy man be poor?
Shall half the new-built Churches round thee fall?
Make Keys, build Bridges, or repair White-hall:
Or to thy Country let that heap be lent,
As M**o's was, but not at five *per Cent*.

   Who thinks that Fortune cannot change her mind,
Prepares a dreadful Jest for all mankind!
And who stands safest, tell me? is it he
That spreads and swells in puff'd Prosperity,
Or blest with little, whose preventing care
In Peace provides fit arms against a War?

   Thus Bethel spoke, who always speaks his thought,
And always thinks the very thing he ought:
His equal mind I copy what I can,
And as I love, would imitate the Man.
In *South-sea* days not happier, when surmis'd
The Lord of thousands, than if now *Excis'd*;
In Forest planted by a Father's hand,
Than in five acres now of rented land.
Content with little, I can piddle here
On Broccoli and mutton, round the year;
But ancient friends, (tho' poor, or out of play)

That touch my Bell, I cannot turn away.
'Tis true, no Turbots dignify my boards,
But gudgeons, flounders, what my Thames affords.
To Hounslow-heath I point, and Bansted-down,
Thence comes your mutton, and these chicks my own:
From yon old wallnut-tree a show'r shall fall;
And grapes, long-lingring on my only wall,
And figs, from standard and Espalier join:
The dev'l is in you if you cannot dine.
Then chearful healths (your Mistress shall have place)
And, what's more rare, a Poet shall say *Grace*.
Fortune not much of humbling me can boast;
Tho' double-tax'd, how little have I lost?
My Life's amusements have been just the same,
Before, and after Standing Armies came.
My lands are sold, my Father's house is gone;
I'll hire another's, is not that my own,
And yours my friends? thro' whose free-opening gate
None comes too early, none departs too late;
(For I, who hold sage Homer's rule the best,
Welcome the coming, speed the going guest.)
'Pray heav'n it last! (cries Swift) as you go on;
I wish to God this house had been your own:
Pity! to build, without a son or wife:
Why, you'll enjoy it only all your life.' –
Well, if the Use be mine, can it concern one
Whether the Name belong to Pope or Vernon?
What's *Property*? dear Swift! you see it alter
From you to me, from me to Peter Walter,
Or, in a mortgage, prove a Lawyer's share,
Or, in a jointure, vanish from the Heir,
Or in pure Equity (the Case not clear)
The Chanc'ry takes your rents for twenty year:
At best, it falls to some ungracious Son
Who cries, my father's damn'd, and all's my own.
Shades, that to Bacon could retreat afford,

Become the portion of a booby Lord;
And Hemsley once proud Buckingham's delight,
Slides to a Scriv'ner or a City Knight.
Let Lands and Houses have what Lords they will,
Let Us be fix'd, and our own Masters still.

from An Imitation of the Sixth Satire of the Second
  Book of Horace
  [*lines 157–223*]

Once on a time (so runs the Fable)
A Country Mouse, right hospitable,
Receiv'd a Town Mouse at his Board,
Just as a Farmer might a Lord.
A frugal Mouse upon the whole,
Yet lov'd his Friend, and had a Soul;
Knew what was handsome, and wou'd do't,
On just occasion, *coute qui coute*.
He brought him Bacon (nothing lean)
Pudding, that might have pleas'd a Dean;
Cheese, such as men in Suffolk make,
But wish'd it Stilton for his sake;
Yet to his Guest tho' no way sparing,
He eat himself the Rind and paring.
Our Courtier scarce could touch a bit,
But show'd his Breeding, and his Wit,
He did his best to seem to eat,
And cry'd, 'I vow you're mighty neat.
As sweet a Cave as one shall see!
A most Romantic hollow Tree!
A pretty kind of savage Scene!
But come, for God's sake, live with Men:
Consider, Mice, like Men, must die,
Both small and great, both you and I:
Then spend your life in Joy and Sport,
(This doctrine, Friend, I learnt at Court.)'
  The veriest Hermit in the Nation
May yield, God knows, to strong Temptation.
Away they come, thro thick and thin,
To a tall house near Lincoln's-Inn:
('Twas on the night of a Debate,

When all their Lordships had sate late.)

    Behold the place, where if a Poet
Shin'd in Description, he might show it,
Tell how the Moon-beam trembling falls
And tips with silver all the walls:
Palladian walls, Venetian doors,
Grotesco roofs, and Stucco floors:
But let it (in a word) be said,
The Moon was up, and Men a-bed,
The Napkins white, the Carpet red:
The Guests withdrawn had left the Treat,
And down the Mice sate, *tête à tête*.

    Our Courtier walks from dish to dish,
Tastes for his Friend of Fowl and Fish;
Tells all their names, lays down the law,
'*Que ça est bon! Ah goutez ça!*
That Jelly's rich, this Malmsey healing,
Pray dip your Whiskers and your Tail in'.
Was ever such a happy Swain?
He stuffs and swills, and stuffs again.
'I'm quite asham'd – 'tis mighty rude
To eat so much – but all's so good.
I have a thousand thanks to give –
My Lord alone knows how to live'.

    No sooner said, but from the Hall
Rush Chaplain, Butler, Dogs and all:
'A Rat, a Rat! clap to the door' –
The Cat comes bouncing on the floor.
O for the Heart of Homer's Mice,
Or Gods to save them in a trice!
(It was by Providence, they think,
For your damn'd Stucco has no chink)
'An't please your Honour, quoth the Peasant,
This same Dessert is not so pleasant:
Give me again my hollow Tree!
A Crust of Bread, and Liberty.'

Sober Advice from Horace, to the Young Gentlemen about Town

The Tribe of Templars, Play'rs, Apothecaries,
Pimps, Poets, Wits, Lord *Fanny*'s, Lady *Mary*'s,
And all the Court in Tears, and half the Town,
Lament dear charming *Oldfield*, dead and gone!
Engaging *Oldfield!* who, with Grace and Ease,
Could joyn the Arts, to ruin, and to please.

Not so, who of Ten Thousand gull'd her Knight,
Then ask'd Ten Thousand for a second Night:
The Gallant too, to whom she pay'd it down,
Liv'd to refuse that Mistress half a Crown.

Con. Philips cries, 'A sneaking Dog I hate.'
That's all three Lovers have for their Estate!
'Treat on, treat on,' is her eternal Note,
And Lands and Tenements go down her Throat.
Some damn the Jade, and some the Cullies blame,
But not Sir *H—t*, for he does the same.

With all a Woman's Virtues but the P—x,
Fufidia thrives in Money, Land, and Stocks:
For Int'rest, ten *per Cent.* her constant Rate is;
Her Body? Hopeful Heirs may have it *gratis*.
She turns her very Sister to a Job,
And, in the Happy Minute, picks your Fob:
Yet starves herself, so little her own Friend,
And thirsts and hungers only at one End:
A Self-Tormentor, worse than (in the Play)
The Wretch, whose Av'rice drove his *Son* away.

But why all this? I'll tell ye, 'tis my Theme:
'Women and Fools are always in Extreme.'
Rufa's at either end a Common-Shoar,
Sweet *Moll* and *Jack* are Civet-Cat and Boar:
Nothing in Nature is so lewd as *Peg*,

Yet, for the World, she would not shew her Leg!
While bashful *Jenny*, ev'n at Morning-Prayer,
Spreads her Fore-Buttocks to the Navel bare.
But diff'rent Taste in diff'rent Men prevails,
And one is fired by Heads, and one by Tails;
Some feel no Flames but at the *Court* or *Ball*,
And others hunt white Aprons in the *Mall*.

My Lord of *L—n*, chancing to remark
A *noted Dean* much busy'd in the Park,
'Proceed (he cry'd) proceed, my Reverend Brother,
'Tis *Fornicatio simplex*, and no other:
Better than lust for Boys, with *Pope* and *Turk*,
Or others Spouses, like my Lord of—'
May no such Praise (cries *J—s*) e'er be mine!
J—s, who bows at *Hi—sb—w*'s *hoary Shrine*.

All you, who think the *City* ne'er can thrive,
Till ev'ry Cuckold-maker's flea'd alive;
Attend, while I their Miseries explain,
And pity Men of Pleasure still in Pain!
Survey the Pangs they bear, the Risques they run,
Where the most lucky are but last undone.
See wretched *Monsieur* flies to save his Throat,
And quits his Mistress, Money, Ring, and Note!
See good Sir *George* of ragged Livery stript,
By worthier Footmen pist upon and whipt!
Plunder'd by Thieves, or Lawyers which is worse,
One bleeds in Person, and one bleeds in Purse;
This meets a Blanket, and that meets a Cudgel –
And all applaud the Justice – All, but *Budgel*.

How much more safe, dear Countrymen! his State,
Who trades in Frigates of the second Rate?
And yet some Care of *S—st* should be had,
Nothing so mean for which he can't run mad;
His Wit confirms him but a Slave the more,
And makes a Princess whom he found a Whore.
The Youth might save much Trouble and Expence,

Were he a Dupe of only common Sense.
But here's his point; 'A Wench (he cries) for me!
I never touch a Dame of Quality.'

To *Palmer*'s Bed no Actress comes amiss,
He courts the whole *Personæ Dramatis:*
He too can say, 'With Wives I never sin.'
But Singing-Girls and Mimicks draw him in.
Sure, worthy Sir, the Diff'rence is not great,
With *whom* you lose your Credit and Estate?
This, or that Person, what avails to shun?
What's wrong is wrong, wherever it be done:
The Ease, Support, and Lustre of your Life,
Destroy'd alike with Strumpet, Maid, or Wife.

What push'd poor *Ellis* on th' Imperial Whore?
'Twas but to be where CHARLES had been before.
The fatal Steel unjustly was apply'd,
When not his Lust offended, but his Pride:
Too hard a Penance for defeated Sin,
Himself shut out, and *Jacob Hall* let in.

Suppose that honest Part that rules us all,
Should rise, and say – 'Sir *Robert!* or Sir *Paul!*
Did I demand, in my most vig'rous hour,
A Thing descended from the Conqueror?
Or when my pulse beat highest, ask for any
Such Nicety, as Lady or Lord *Fanny?*' –
What would you answer? Could you have the Face,
When the poor Suff'rer humbly mourn'd his Case,
To cry 'You weep the Favours of her GRACE?'

Hath not indulgent Nature spread a Feast,
And giv'n enough for Man, enough for Beast?
But Man corrupt, perverse in all his ways,
In search of Vanities from Nature strays:
Yea, tho' the Blessing's more than he can use,
Shun the permitted, the forbid pursues!
Weigh well the Cause from whence these Evils spring,
'Tis in thyself, and not in God's good Thing:

Then, lest Repentence punish such a Life,
Never, ah, never! kiss thy Neighbour's Wife.

   First, Silks and Diamonds veil no finer Shape,
Or plumper Thigh, than lurk in humble Crape:
And *secondly*, how innocent a *Belle*
Is she who shows what Ware she has to sell;
Not Lady-like, displays a milk-white Breast,
And hides in sacred Sluttishness the rest.

   Our ancient Kings (and sure those Kings were wise,
Who judg'd themselves, and saw with their own Eyes)
A War-horse never for the Service chose,
But ey'd him round, and stript off all the Cloaths;
For well they knew, proud Trappings serve to hide
A heavy Chest, thick Neck, or heaving Side.
But Fools are ready Chaps, agog to buy,
Let but a comely Fore-hand strike the Eye:
No Eagle sharper, every Charm to find,
To all defects, *Ty—y* not so blind:
Goose-rump'd, Hawk-nos'd, Swan-footed, is my Dear?
They'l praise her *Elbow*, *Heel*, or *Tip o' th' Ear*.

   A Lady's Face is all you see undress'd;
(For none but Lady M— shows the Rest)
But if to Charms more latent you pretend,
What Lines encompass, and what Works defend!
Dangers on Dangers! obstacles by dozens!
Spies, Guardians, Guests, old Women, Aunts, and Cozens!
Could you directly to her Person go,   ⎫
Stays will obstruct above, and Hoops below,   ⎬
And if the Dame says yes, the Dress says no.   ⎭
Not thus at *N—dh—m*'s; your judicious Eye
May measure there the Breast, the Hip, the Thigh!
And will you run to Perils, Sword, and Law,
All for a Thing you ne're so much as *saw?*

   'The Hare once seiz'd the Hunter heeds no more
The little Scut he so pursu'd before,
Love follows flying Game (as *Sucklyn* sings)

And 'tis for that the wanton Boy has Wings.'
Why let him Sing—but when you're in the Wrong,
Think ye to cure the Mischief with a Song?
Has Nature set no bounds to wild Desire?
No Sense to guide, no Reason to enquire,
What solid Happiness, what empty Pride?
And what is best indulg'd, or best deny'd?
If neither Gems adorn, nor Silver tip
The flowing Bowl, will you not wet your Lip?
When sharp with Hunger, scorn you to be fed,
Except on *Pea-Chicks*, at the *Bedford-head*?
Or, when a tight, neat Girl, will serve the Turn,
In errant Pride continue stiff, and burn?
I'm a plain Man, whose Maxim is profest,
'The Thing at hand is of all Things the *best*.'
But Her who will, and then will not comply,
Whose Word is *If, Perhaps*, and *By-and-By*,
Z—ds! let some Eunuch or Platonic take –
So *B—t* cries, Philosopher and Rake!
Who asks no more (right reasonable Peer)
Than not to wait too long, nor pay too dear.
Give me a willing Nymph! 'tis all I care,
Extremely clean, and tolerably fair,
Her Shape her own, whatever Shape she have,
And just that White and Red which Nature gave.
Her I transported touch, transported view,
And call her *Angel! Goddess! Montague!*
No furious Husband thunders at the Door;
No barking Dog, no Household in a Roar;
From gleaming Swords no shrieking Women run;
No wretched Wife cries out, *Undone! Undone?*
Seiz'd in the Fact, and in her Cuckold's Pow'r,
She kneels, she weeps, and worse! resigns her Dow'r.
Me, naked me, to Posts, to Pumps they draw,
To Shame eternal, or eternal Law.

The First Ode of the Fourth Book of Horace,
To Venus

Again? new Tumults in my Breast?
Ah spare me, Venus! let me, let me rest!
   I am not now, alas! the man
As in the gentle Reign of My Queen *Anne.*
     Ah sound no more thy soft alarms,
Nor circle sober fifty with thy Charms.
    Mother too fierce of dear Desires!
Turn, turn to willing Hearts your wanton fires.
    To *Number five* direct your Doves,
There spread round MURRAY all your blooming Loves;
    Noble and young, who strikes the heart
With every sprightly, every decent part;
    Equal, the injur'd to defend,
To charm the Mistress, or to fix the Friend.
    He, with a hundred Arts refin'd,
Shall stretch thy Conquests over half the kind:
    To him each Rival shall submit,
Make but his riches equal to his Wit.
    Then shall thy Form the Marble grace,
(Thy Græcian Form) and Chloe lend the Face:
    His House, embosom'd in the Grove,
Sacred to social Life and social Love,
    Shall glitter o'er the pendent green,
Where Thames reflects the visionary Scene.
    Thither, the silver-sounding Lyres
Shall call the smiling Loves, and young Desires;
    There, every Grace and Muse shall throng,
Exalt the Dance, or animate the Song;
    There, Youths and Nymphs, in consort gay,
Shall hail the rising, close the parting day.
    With me, alas! those joys are o'er;
For me, the vernal Garlands bloom no more.

Adieu! fond hope of mutual fire,
The still-believing, still-renew'd desire;
    Adieu! the heart-expanding bowl,
And all the kind Deceivers of the soul!
    – But why? ah tell me, ah too dear!
Steals down my cheek th' involuntary Tear?
    Why words so flowing, thoughts so free,
Stop, or turn nonsense at one glance of Thee?
    Thee, drest in Fancy's airy beam,
Absent I follow thro' th' extended Dream,
    Now, now I seize, I clasp thy charms,
And now you burst, (ah cruel!) from my arms,
    And swiftly shoot along the Mall,
    Or softly glide by the Canal,
    Now shown by Cynthia's silver Ray,
And now, on rolling Waters snatch'd away.

from The Dunciad in Four Books
[*Book IV*]

Yet, yet a moment, one dim Ray of Light
Indulge, dread Chaos, and eternal Night!
Of darkness visible so much be lent,
As half to shew, half veil the deep Intent.
Ye Pow'rs! whose Mysteries restor'd I sing,
To whom Time bears me on his rapid wing,
Suspend a while your Force inertly strong,
Then take at once the Poet and the Song.

    Now flam'd the Dog-star's unpropitious ray,
Smote ev'ry Brain, and wither'd ev'ry Bay;
Sick was the Sun, the Owl forsook his bow'r,
The moon-struck Prophet felt the madding hour:
Then rose the Seed of Chaos, and of Night,
To blot out Order, and extinguish Light,
Of dull and venal a new World to mold,
And bring Saturnian days of Lead and Gold.

    She mounts the Throne: her head a Cloud conceal'd,
In broad Effulgence all below reveal'd,
('Tis thus aspiring Dulness ever shines)
Soft on her lap her Laureat son reclines.

    Beneath her foot-stool, *Science* groans in Chains,
And *Wit* dreads Exile, Penalties and Pains.
There foam'd rebellious *Logic*, gagg'd and bound,
There, stript, fair *Rhet'ric* languish'd on the ground;
His blunted Arms by *Sophistry* are born,
And shameless *Billingsgate* her Robes adorn.
Morality, by her false Guardians drawn,
Chicane in Furs, and *Casuistry* in Lawn,
Gasps, as they straiten at each end the cord,
And dies, when Dulness gives her Page the word.
Mad *Mathesis* alone was unconfin'd,
Too mad for mere material chains to bind,

Now to pure Space lifts her extatic stare,
Now running round the Circle, finds it square.
But held in ten-fold bonds the *Muses* lie,
Watch'd both by Envy's and by Flatt'ry's eye:
There to her heart sad Tragedy addrest
The dagger wont to pierce the Tyrant's breast;
But sober History restrain'd her rage,
And promis'd Vengeance on a barb'rous age.
There sunk Thalia, nerveless, cold, and dead,
Had not her Sister Satyr held her head:
Nor cou'd'st thou, CHESTERFIELD! a tear refuse,
Thou wept'st, and with thee wept each gentle Muse.

　　When lo! a Harlot form soft sliding by,
With mincing step, small voice, and languid eye;
Foreign her air, her robe's discordant pride
In patch-work flutt'ring, and her head aside.
By singing Peers up-held on either hand,
She tripp'd and laugh'd, too pretty much to stand;
Cast on the prostrate Nine a scornful look;
Then thus in quaint Recitativo spoke.

　　'O *Cara! Cara!* silence all that train:
Joy to great Chaos! let Division reign:
Chromatic tortures soon shall drive them hence,
Break all their nerves, and fritter all their sense:
One Trill shall harmonize joy, grief, and rage,
Wake the dull Church, and lull the ranting Stage;
To the same notes thy sons shall hum, or snore,
And all thy yawning daughters cry, *encore.*
Another Phœbus, thy own Phœbus, reigns,
Joys in my jiggs, and dances in my chains.
But soon, ah soon Rebellion will commence,
If Music meanly borrows aid from Sense.
Strong in new Arms, lo! Giant Handel stands,
Like bold Briareus, with a hundred hands;
To stir, to rouze, to shake the Soul he comes,
And Jove's own Thunders follow Mars's Drums.

Arrest him, Empress; or you sleep no more' –
She heard, and drove him to th' Hibernian shore.

   And now had Fame's posterior Trumpet blown,
And all the Nations summon'd to the Throne.
The young, the old, who feel her inward sway,
One instinct seizes, and transports away.
None need a guide, by sure Attraction led,
And strong impulsive gravity of Head:
None want a place, for all their Centre found,
Hung to the Goddess, and coher'd around.
Not closer, orb in orb, conglob'd are seen
The buzzing Bees about their dusky Queen.

   The gath'ring number, as it moves along,
Involves a vast involuntary throng,
Who gently drawn, and struggling less and less,
Roll in her Vortex, and her pow'r confess.
Not those alone who passive own her laws,
But who, weak rebels, more advance her cause.
Whate'er of dunce in College or in Town
Sneers at another, in toupee or gown;
Whate'er of mungril no one class admits,
A wit with dunces, and a dunce with wits.

   Nor absent they, no members of her state,
Who pay her homage in her sons, the Great;
Who false to Phœbus, bow the knee to Baal;
Or impious, preach his Word without a call.
Patrons, who sneak from living worth to dead,
With-hold the pension, and set up the head;
Or vest dull Flatt'ry in the sacred Gown;
Or give from fool to fool the Laurel crown.
And (last and worst) with all the cant of wit,
Without the soul, the Muse's Hypocrit.

   There march'd the bard and blockhead, side by side,
Who rhym'd for hire, and patroniz'd for pride.
Narcissus, prais'd with all a Parson's pow'r,
Look'd a white lilly sunk beneath a show'r.

There mov'd Montalto with superior air;
His stretch'd-out arm display'd a Volume fair;
Courtiers and Patriots in two ranks divide,
Thro' both he pass'd, and bow'd from side to side:
But as in graceful act, with awful eye
Compos'd he stood, bold Benson thrust him by:
On two unequal crutches propt he came,
Milton's on this, on that one Johnston's name.
The decent Knight retir'd with sober rage,
Withdrew his hand, and clos'd the pompous page.
[But (happy for him as the times went then)
Appear'd Apollo's May'r and Aldermen,
On whom three hundred gold-capt youths await,
To lug the pond'rous volume off in state.]

   When Dulness, smiling – 'Thus revive the Wits!
But murder first, and mince them all to bits;
As erst Medea (cruel, so to save!)
A new Edition of old Æson gave,
Let standard-Authors, thus, like trophies born,
Appear more glorious as more hack'd and torn,
And you, my Critics! in the chequer'd shade,
Admire new light thro' holes yourselves have made.

   'Leave not a foot of verse, a foot of stone,
A Page, a Grave, that they can call their own;
But spread, my sons, your glory thin or thick,
On passive paper, or on solid brick.
So by each Bard an Alderman shall sit,
A heavy Lord shall hang at ev'ry Wit,
And while on Fame's triumphal Car they ride,
Some Slave of mind be pinion'd to their side.'

   Now crowds on crowds around the Goddess press,
Each eager to present the first Address.
Dunce scorning Dunce beholds the next advance,
But Fop shews Fop superior complaisance.
When lo! a Spectre rose, whose index-hand
Held forth the Virtue of the dreadful wand;

His beaver'd brow a birchen garland wears,
Dropping with Infant's blood, and Mother's tears.
O'er ev'ry vein a shudd'ring horror runs;
Eton and Winton shake thro' all their Sons.
All Flesh is humbled, Westminster's bold race
Shrink, and confess the Genius of the place:
The pale Boy-Senator yet tingling stands,
And holds his breeches close with both his hands.

   Then thus. 'Since Man from beast by Words is known,
Words are Man's province, Words we teach alone.
When Reason doubtful, like the Samian letter,
Points him two ways, the narrower is the better.
Plac'd at the door of Learning, youth to guide,
We never suffer it to stand too wide.
To ask, to guess, to know, as they commence,
As Fancy opens the quick springs of Sense,
We ply the Memory, we load the brain,
Bind rebel Wit, and double chain on chain,
Confine the thought, to exercise the breath;
And keep them in the pale of Words till death.
Whate'er the talents, or howe'er design'd,
We hang one jingling padlock on the mind:
A Poet the first day, he dips his quill;
And what the last? a very Poet still.
Pity! the charm works only in our wall,
Lost, lost too soon in yonder House or Hall.
There truant WYNDHAM ev'ry Muse gave o'er,
There TALBOT sunk, and was a Wit no more!
How sweet an Ovid, MURRAY was our boast!
How many Martials were in PULT'NEY lost!
Else sure some Bard, to our eternal praise,
In twice ten thousand rhyming nights and days,
Had reach'd the Work, the All that mortal can;
And South beheld that Master-piece of Man.'
'Oh (cry'd the Goddess) for some pedant Reign!
Some gentle JAMES, to bless the land again;

To stick the Doctor's Chair into the Throne,
Give law to Words, or war with Words alone,
Senates and Courts with Greek and Latin rule,
And turn the Council to a Grammar School!
For sure, if Dulness sees a grateful Day,
'Tis in the shade of Arbitrary Sway.
O! if my sons may learn one earthly thing,
Teach but that one, sufficient for a King;
That which my Priests, and mine alone, maintain,
Which as it dies, or lives, we fall, or reign:
May you, may Cam, and Isis preach it long!
"The RIGHT DIVINE of Kings to govern wrong." '

   Prompt at the call, around the Goddess roll
Broad hats, and hoods, and caps, a sable shoal:
Thick and more thick the black blockade extends,
A hundred head of Aristotle's friends.
Nor wert thou, Isis! wanting to the day,
[Tho' Christ-church long kept prudishly away.]
Each staunch Polemic, stubborn as a rock,
Each fierce Logician, still expelling Locke,
Came whip and spur, and dash'd thro' thin and thick
On German Crouzaz, and Dutch Burgersdyck.
As many quit the streams that murm'ring fall
To lull the sons of Marg'ret and Clare-hall,
Where Bentley late tempestuous wont to sport
In troubled waters, but now sleeps in Port.
Before them march'd that awful Aristarch;
Plow'd was his front with many a deep Remark:
His Hat, which never vail'd to human pride,
Walker with rev'rence took, and lay'd aside.
Low bow'd the rest: He, kingly, did but nod;
So upright Quakers please both Man and God.
'Mistress! dismiss that rabble from your throne:
Avaunt——is Aristarchus yet unknown?
Thy mighty Scholiast, whose unweary'd pains
Made Horace dull, and humbled Milton's strains.

Turn what they will to Verse, their toil is vain,
Critics like me shall make it Prose again.
Roman and Greek Grammarians! know your Better:
Author of something yet more great than Letter;
While tow'ring o'er your Alphabet, like Saul,
Stands our Digamma, and o'er-tops them all.
'Tis true, on Words is still our whole debate,
Disputes of *Me* or *Te*, of *aut* or *at*,
To sound or sink in *cano*, O or A,
Or give up Cicero to C or K.
Let Freind affect to speak as Terence spoke,
And Alsop never but like Horace joke:
For me, what Virgil, Pliny may deny,
Manilius or Solinus shall supply:
For Attic Phrase in Plato let them seek,
I poach in Suidas for unlicens'd Greek.
In ancient Sense if any needs will deal,
Be sure I give them Fragments, not a Meal;
What Gellius or Stobæus hash'd before,
Or chew'd by blind old Scholiasts o'er and o'er.
The critic Eye, that microscope of Wit,
Sees hairs and pores, examines bit by bit:
How parts relate to parts, or they to whole,
The body's harmony, the beaming soul,
Are things which Kuster, Burman, Wasse shall see,
When Man's whole frame is obvious to a *Flea*.

'Ah, think not, Mistress! more true Dulness lies
In Folly's Cap, than Wisdom's grave disguise.
Like buoys, that never sink into the flood,
On Learning's surface we but lie and nod.
Thine is the genuine head of many a house,
And much Divinity without a Νοῦς.
Nor could a BARROW work on ev'ry block,
Nor has one ATTERBURY spoil'd the flock.
See! still thy own, the heavy Canon roll,
And Metaphysic smokes involve the Pole.

For thee we dim the eyes, and stuff the head
With all such reading as was never read:
For thee explain a thing till all men doubt it,
And write about it, Goddess, and about it:
So spins the silk-worm small its slender store,
And labours till it clouds itself all o'er.

   'What tho' we let some better sort of fool
Thrid ev'ry science, run thro' ev'ry school?
Never by tumbler thro' the hoops was shown
Such skill in passing all, and touching none.
He may indeed (if sober all this time)
Plague with Dispute, or persecute with Rhyme.
We only furnish what he cannot use,
Or wed to what he must divorce, a Muse:
Full in the midst of Euclid dip at once,
And petrify a Genius to a Dunce:
Or set on Metaphysic ground to prance,
Show all his paces, not a step advance.
With the same Cement, ever sure to bind,
We bring to one dead level ev'ry mind.
Then take him to devellop, if you can,
And hew the Block off, and get out the Man.
But wherefore waste I words? I see advance
Whore, Pupil, and lac'd Governor from France.
Walker! our hat' – nor more he deign'd to say,
But, stern as Ajax' spectre, strode away.

   In flow'd at once a gay embroider'd race,
And titt'ring push'd the Pedants off the place:
Some would have spoken, but the voice was drown'd
By the French horn, or by the op'ning hound.
The first came forwards, with as easy mien,
As if he saw St. James's and the Queen.
When thus th' attendant Orator begun.
'Receive, great Empress! thy accomplish'd Son:
Thine from the birth, and sacred from the rod,
A dauntless infant! never scar'd with God.

The Sire saw, one by one, his Virtues wake:
The Mother begg'd the blessing of a Rake.
Thou gav'st that Ripeness, which so soon began,
And ceas'd so soon, he ne'er was Boy, nor Man.
Thro' School and College, thy kind cloud o'ercast,
Safe and unseen the young Æneas past:
Thence bursting glorious, all at once let down,
Stunn'd with his giddy Larum half the town.
Intrepid then, o'er seas and lands he flew:
Europe he saw, and Europe saw him too.
There all thy gifts and graces we display,
Thou, only thou, directing all our way!
To where the Seine, obsequious as she runs,
Pours at great Bourbon's feet her silken sons;
Or Tyber, now no longer Roman, rolls,
Vain of Italian Arts, Italian Souls:
To happy Convents, bosom'd deep in vines,
Where slumber Abbots, purple as their wines:
To Isles of fragrance, lilly-silver'd vales,
Diffusing languor in the panting gales:
To lands of singing, or of dancing slaves,
Love-whisp'ring woods, and lute-resounding waves.
But chief her shrine where naked Venus keeps,
And Cupids ride the Lyon of the Deeps;
Where, eas'd of Fleets, the Adriatic main
Wafts the smooth Eunuch and enamour'd swain.
Led by my hand, he saunter'd Europe round,
And gather'd ev'ry Vice on Christian ground;
Saw ev'ry Court, heard ev'ry King declare
His royal Sense, of Op'ra's or the Fair;
The Stews and Palace equally explor'd,
Intrigu'd with glory, and with spirit whor'd;
Try'd all *hors-d'œuvres*, all *liqueurs* defin'd;
Judicious drank, and greatly-daring din'd;
Dropt the dull lumber of the Latin store,
Spoil'd his own language, and acquir'd no more;

All Classic learning lost on Classic ground;
And last turn'd *Air*, the Echo of a Sound!
See now, half-cur'd, and perfectly well-bred,
With nothing but a Solo in his head;
As much Estate, and Principle, and Wit,
As Jansen, Fleetwood, Cibber shall think fit;
Stol'n from a Duel, follow'd by a Nun,
And, if a Borough chuse him, not undone;
See, to my country happy I restore
This glorious Youth, and add one Venus more.
Her too receive (for her my soul adores)
So may the sons of sons of sons of whores,
Prop thine, O Empress! like each neighbour Throne,
And make a long Posterity thy own.'

    Pleas'd, she accepts the Hero, and the Dame,
Wraps in her Veil, and frees from sense of Shame.

    Then look'd, and saw a lazy, lolling sort,
Unseen at Church, at Senate, or at Court,
Of ever-listless Loit'rers, that attend
No cause, no Trust, no Duty, and no Friend.
Thee too, my Paridel! she mark'd thee there,
Stretch'd on the rack of a too easy chair,
And heard thy everlasting yawn confess
The Pains and Penalties of Idleness.
She pity'd! but her Pity only shed
Benigner influence on thy nodding head.

    But Annius, crafty Seer, with ebon wand,
And well dissembled em'rald on his hand,
False as his Gems, and canker'd as his Coins,
Came, cramm'd with capon, from where Pollio dines.
Soft, as the wily Fox is seen to creep,
Where bask on sunny banks the simple sheep,
Walk round and round, now prying here, now there;
So he; but pious, whisper'd first his pray'r.

    'Grant, gracious Goddess! grant me still to cheat,
O may thy cloud still cover the deceit!

Thy choicer mists on this assembly shed,
But pour them thickest on the noble head.
So shall each youth, assisted by our eyes,
See other Cæsars, other Homers rise;
Thro' twilight ages hunt th' Athenian fowl,
Which Chalcis Gods, and mortals call an Owl,
Now see an Attys, now a Cecrops clear,
Nay, Mahomet! the Pigeon at thine ear;
Be rich in ancient brass, tho' not in gold,
And keep his Lares, tho' his house be sold;
To headless Phœbe his fair bride postpone,
Honour a Syrian Prince above his own;
Lord of an Otho, if I vouch it true;
Blest in one Niger, till he knows of two.'

   Mummius o'erheard him; Mummius, Fool-renown'd,
Who like his Cheops stinks above the ground,
Fierce as a startled Adder, swell'd, and said,
Rattling an ancient Sistrum at his head.

   'Speak'st thou of Syrian Princes? Traitor base!
Mine, Goddess! mine is all the horned race.
True, he had wit, to make their value rise;
From foolish Greeks to steal them, was as wise;
More glorious yet, from barb'rous hands to keep,
When Sallee Rovers chac'd him on the deep.
Then taught by Hermes, and divinely bold,
Down his own throat he risqu'd the Grecian gold;
Receiv'd each Demi-God, with pious care,
Deep in his Entrails – I rever'd them there,
I bought them, shrouded in that living shrine,
And, at their second birth, they issue mine.'

   'Witness great Ammon! by whose horns I swore,
(Reply'd soft Annius) this our paunch before
Still bears them, faithful; and that thus I eat,
Is to refund the Medals with the meat.
To prove me, Goddess! clear of all design,
Bid me with Pollio sup, as well as dine:

There all the Learn'd shall at the labour stand,
And Douglas lend his soft, obstetric hand.'

The Goddess smiling seem'd to give consent;
So back to Pollio, hand in hand, they went.

Then thick as Locusts black'ning all the ground,
A tribe, with weeds and shells fantastic crown'd,
Each with some wond'rous gift approach'd the Pow'r,
A Nest, a Toad, a Fungus, or a Flow'r.
But far the foremost, two, with earnest zeal,
And aspect ardent to the Throne appeal.

The first thus open'd: 'Hear thy suppliant's call,
Great Queen, and common Mother of us all!
Fair from its humble bed I rear'd this Flow'r,
Suckled, and chear'd, with air, and sun, and show'r,
Soft on the paper ruff its leaves I spread,
Bright with the gilded button tipt its head,
Then thron'd in glass, and nam'd it CAROLINE:
Each Maid cry'd, charming! and each Youth, divine!
Did Nature's pencil ever blend such rays,
Such vary'd light in one promiscuous blaze?
Now prostrate! dead! behold that Caroline:
No Maid cries, charming! and no Youth, divine!
And lo the wretch! whose vile, whose insect lust
Lay'd this gay daughter of the Spring in dust.
Oh punish him, or to th' Elysian shades
Dismiss my soul, where no Carnation fades.'

He ceas'd, and wept. With innocence of mein,
Th' Accus'd stood forth, and thus address'd the Queen.

'Of all th' enamel'd race, whose silv'ry wing
Waves to the tepid Zephyrs of the spring,
Or swims along the fluid atmosphere,
Once brightest shin'd this child of Heat and Air.
I saw, and started from its vernal bow'r
The rising game, and chac'd from flow'r to flow'r.
It fled, I follow'd; now in hope, now pain;
It stopt, I stopt; it mov'd, I mov'd again.

At last it fix'd, 'twas on what plant it pleas'd,
And where it fix'd, the beauteous bird I seiz'd:
Rose or Carnation was below my care;
I meddle, Goddess! only in my sphere.
I tell the naked fact without disguise,
And, to excuse it, need but shew the prize;
Whose spoils this paper offers to your eye,
Fair ev'n in death! this peerless *Butterfly*.'

'My sons! (she answer'd) both have done your parts:
Live happy both, and long promote our arts.
But hear a Mother, when she recommends
To your fraternal care, our sleeping friends.
The common Soul, of Heav'n's more frugal make,
Serves but to keep fools pert, and knaves awake:
A drowzy Watchman, that just gives a knock,
And breaks our rest, to tell us what's a clock.
Yet by some object ev'ry brain is stirr'd;
The dull may waken to a Humming-bird;
The most recluse, discreetly open'd find
Congenial matter in the Cockle-kind;
The mind, in Metaphysics at a loss,
May wander in a wilderness of Moss;
The head that turns at super-lunar things,
Poiz'd with a tail, may steer on Wilkins' wings.

'O! would the Sons of Men once think their Eyes
And Reason giv'n them but to study *Flies*?
See Nature in some partial narrow shape,
And let the Author of the Whole escape:
Learn but to trifle; or, who most observe,
To wonder at their Maker, not to serve.'

'Be that my task (replies a gloomy Clerk,
Sworn foe to Myst'ry, yet divinely dark;
Whose pious hope aspires to see the day
When Moral Evidence shall quite decay,
And damns implicit faith, and holy lies,
Prompt to impose, and fond to dogmatize:)

Let others creep by timid steps, and slow,
On plain Experience lay foundations low,
By common sense to common knowledge bred,
And last, to Nature's Cause thro' Nature led.
All-seeing in thy mists, we want no guide,
Mother of Arrogance, and Source of Pride!
We nobly take the high Priori Road,
And reason downward, till we doubt of God:
Make Nature still incroach upon his plan;
And shove him off as far as e'er we can:
Thrust some Mechanic Cause into his place;
Or bind in Matter, or diffuse in Space.
Or, at one bound o'er-leaping all his laws,
Make God Man's Image, Man the final Cause,
Find Virtue local, all Relation scorn,
See all in *Self*, and but for self be born:
Of nought so certain as our *Reason* still,
Of nought so doubtful as of *Soul* and *Will*.
Oh hide the God still more! and make us see
Such as Lucretius drew, a God like Thee:
Wrapt up in Self, a God without a Thought,
Regardless of our merit or default.
Or that bright Image to our fancy draw,
Which Theocles in raptur'd vision saw,
While thro' Poetic scenes the Genius roves,
Or wanders wild in Academic Groves;
That NATURE our Society adores,
Where Tindal dictates, and Silenus snores.'

   Rous'd at his name, up rose the bowzy Sire,
And shook from out his Pipe the seeds of fire;
Then snapt his box, and strok'd his belly down:
Rosy and rev'rend, tho' without a Gown.
Bland and familiar to the throne he came,
Led up the Youth, and call'd the Goddess *Dame*.
Then thus. 'From Priest-craft happily set free,
Lo! ev'ry finish'd Son returns to thee:

First slave to Words, then vassal to a Name,
Then dupe to Party; child and man the same;
Bounded by Nature, narrow'd still by Art,
A trifling head, and a contracted heart.
Thus bred, thus taught, how many have I seen,
Smiling on all, and smil'd on by a Queen.
Mark'd out for Honours, honour'd for their Birth,
To thee the most rebellious things on earth:
Now to thy gentle shadow all are shrunk,
All melted down, in Pension, or in Punk!
So K * so B * * sneak'd into the grave,
A Monarch's half, and half a Harlot's slave.
Poor W * * nipt in Folly's broadest bloom,
Who praises now? his Chaplain on his Tomb.
Then take them all, oh take them to thy breast!
Thy *Magus*, Goddess! shall perform the rest.'
  With that, a WIZARD OLD his *Cup* extends;
Which who so tastes, forgets his former friends,
Sire, Ancestors, Himself. One casts his eyes
Up to a *Star*, and like Endymion dies:
A *Feather* shooting from another's head,
Extracts his brain, and Principle is fled,
Lost is his God, his Country, ev'ry thing;
And nothing left but Homage to a King!
The vulgar herd turn off to roll with Hogs,
To run with Horses, or to hunt with Dogs;
But, sad example! never to escape
Their Infamy, still keep the human shape.
  But she, good Goddess, sent to ev'ry child
Firm Impudence, or Stupefaction mild;
And strait succeeded, leaving shame no room,
Cibberian forehead, or Cimmerian gloom.
  Kind Self-conceit to some her glass applies,
Which no one looks in with another's eyes:
But as the Flatt'rer or Dependent paint,
Beholds himself a Patriot, Chief, or Saint.

On others Int'rest her gay liv'ry flings,
Int'rest, that waves on Party-colour'd wings:
Turn'd to the Sun, she casts a thousand dyes,
And, as she turns, the colours fall or rise.
Others the Syren Sisters warble round,
And empty heads console with empty sound.
No more, alas! the voice of Fame they hear,
The balm of Dulness trickling in their ear.
Great C * *, H * *, P * *, R * *, K *,
Why all your Toils? your Sons have learn'd to sing.
How quick Ambition hastes to ridicule!
The Sire is made a Peer, the Son a Fool.
On some, a Priest succinct in amice white
Attends; all flesh is nothing in his sight!
Beeves, at his touch, at once to jelly turn,
And the huge Boar is shrunk into an Urn:
The board with specious miracles he loads,
Turns Hares to Larks, and Pigeons into Toads.
Another (for in all what one can shine?)
Explains the *Seve* and *Verdeur* of the Vine.
What cannot copious Sacrifice attone?
Thy Treufles, Perigord! thy Hams, Bayonne!
With French Libation, and Italian Strain,
Wash Bladen white, and expiate Hays's stain.
Knight lifts the head, for what are crowds undone
To three essential Partriges in one?
Gone ev'ry blush, and silent all reproach,
Contending Princes mount them in their Coach.
    Next bidding all draw near on bended knees,
The Queen confers her *Titles* and *Degrees*.
Her children first of more distinguish'd sort,
Who study Shakespeare at the Inns of Court,
Impale a Glow-worm, or Vertù profess,
Shine in the dignity of F. R. S.
Some, deep Free-Masons, join the silent race
Worthy to fill Pythagoras's place:

Some Botanists, or Florists at the least,
Or issue Members of an Annual feast.
Nor past the meanest unregarded, one
Rose a Gregorian, one a Gormogon.
The last, not least in honour or applause,
Isis and Cam made Doctors of her Laws.
   Then blessing all, 'Go Children of my care!
To Practice now from Theory repair.
All my commands are easy, short and full:
My Sons! be proud, be selfish, and be dull.
Guard my Prerogative, assert my Throne:
This Nod confirms each Privilege your own.
The Cap and Switch be sacred to his Grace;
With Staff and Pumps the Marquis lead the Race;
From Stage to Stage the licens'd Earl may run,
Pair'd with his Fellow-Charioteer the Sun;
The learned Baron Butterflies design,
Or draw to silk Arachne's subtile line;
The Judge to dance his brother Sergeant call;
The Senator at Cricket urge the Ball;
The Bishop stow (Pontific Luxury!)
An hundred Souls of Turkeys in a pye;
The sturdy Squire to Gallic masters stoop,
And drown his Lands and Manors in a Soupe.
Others import yet nobler arts from France,
Teach Kings to fiddle, and make Senates dance.
Perhaps more high some daring son may soar,
Proud to my list to add one Monarch more;
And nobly conscious, Princes are but things
Born for First Ministers, as Slaves for Kings,
Tyrant supreme! shall three Estates command,
And MAKE ONE MIGHTY DUNCIAD OF THE LAND!'
   More she had spoke, but yawn'd – All Nature nods:
What Mortal can resist the Yawn of Gods?
Churches and Chapels instantly it reach'd;
(St. James's first, for leaden Gilbert preach'd)

Then catch'd the Schools; the Hall scarce kept awake;
The Convocation gap'd, but could not speak:
Lost was the Nation's Sense, nor could be found,
While the long solemn Unison went round:
Wide, and more wide, it spread o'er all the realm;
Ev'n Palinurus nodded at the Helm:
The Vapour mild o'er each Committee crept;
Unfinish'd Treaties in each Office slept;
And Chiefless Armies doz'd out the Campaign;
And Navies yawn'd for Orders on the Main.

   O Muse! relate (for you can tell alone,
Wits have short Memories, and Dunces none)
Relate, who first, who last resign'd to rest;
Whose Heads she partly, whose completely blest;
What Charms could Faction, what Ambition lull,
The Venal quiet, and intrance the Dull;
'Till drown'd was Sense, and Shame, and Right, and Wrong –
O sing, and hush the Nations with thy Song!

     *   *   *   *   *   *

   In vain, in vain, – the all-composing Hour
Resistless falls: The Muse obeys the Pow'r.
She comes! she comes! the sable Throne behold
Of *Night* Primæval, and of *Chaos* old!
Before her, *Fancy's* gilded clouds decay,
And all its varying Rain-bows die away.
Wit shoots in vain its momentary fires,
The meteor drops, and in a flash expires.
As one by one, at dread Medea's strain,
The sick'ning stars fade off th' ethereal plain;
As Argus' eyes by Hermes' wand opprest,
Clos'd one by one to everlasting rest;
Thus at her felt approach, and secret might,
Art after *Art* goes out, and all is Night.
See skulking *Truth* to her old Cavern fled,
Mountains of Casuistry heap'd o'er her head!

Philosophy, that lean'd on Heav'n before,
Shrinks to her second cause, and is no more.
Physic of *Metaphysic* begs defence,
And *Metaphysic* calls for aid on *Sense*!
See *Mystery* to *Mathematics* fly!
In vain! they gaze, turn giddy, rave, and die.
Religion blushing veils her sacred fires,
And unawares *Morality* expires.
Nor *public* Flame, nor *private*, dares to shine;
Nor *human* Spark is left, nor Glimpse *divine*!
Lo! thy dread Empire, Chaos! is restor'd;
Light dies before thy uncreating word:
Thy hand, great Anarch! lets the curtain fall;
And Universal Darkness buries All.